ILLUSTRATED
TRANSPORTATION

平尾 收
Osamu Hirao

『日本人の器用さとセンスの成果』

　JAAAが結成されたのは'79年の7月だったから，すでに7年が経過しました。自動車を中心とする現在の第一線に活躍中のアーティストたちの集団とはいいながら，そのレパートリーは広く，海や空のあらゆるビークルはもちろん，電子機器やカメラその他の精密機器類にまで及び，およそ工業製品の花形たちのスケルトンをよくこなし，また，困難なムードの表現など，その成果は年を追って業界の驚異となりつつあり，今や世界一流の名声を博しつつある。これらは日本人特有の繊細さと美的センス，加えてたゆみない努力の結晶と信じ，大いに世界に誇りたいと思っています。

　だが，この集団の各人は同じ道を行く者同士，裏を返せば呉越同舟，きびしく相手を意識するライバル同士なのだ。しかしそれを逆手にとってお互いに技を磨き合い，和気あいあいと運営され，会員も年とともに増えつつあるということは，この種の集団としてはきわめて異例かもしれない。

　また，JAAAの価値を高く評価され，イラスト展その他でいろいろと御協力下さる企業の方々により，日頃の成果の発表の場を広く与えていただいたことは会員にとって何よりの喜びであると同時に，他の多くのイラストレーターやその予備軍たち，あわせて出版関係の方たちにも多大の影響をもたらしていることになり，我々の大きな目標のひとつがかなえられていると，幾重にも感謝しています。

　さらにこの度，美術出版として高名，実績の高い株式会社グラフィック社の御好意により，しかも初のビークルすなわち乗物だけを特集した豪華なカラー版にJAAA会員の全力を披露させていただくことになったことは大きな喜びです。そしてまた，この企画に御協力下さった幾多のゲストの方たちに深甚なる謝意を表する次第です。

　最後に，これからこうしたインダストリアル・アーティストの世界に進もうとする多くの若きイラストレーターの方たちに大いに期待と楽しみを抱きながら，この書が何らかの新しい創造的発想の引き金をもたらすことができましたら，これに過ぎるものはありません。

JAAA会長
東大名誉教授

片山 豊
Yutaka Katayama

『足跡進歩の記録』

　皆さんの努力でカラーイラスト集の豪華版が出版される事になった事は大変お目出たい事です。展覧会という一つの会場で皆さんが顔を合せ努力して数日間の展示が行われる事はそれだけ重要な意義があるとしても，それぞれの作品が集大成されて，繰返しの観賞に提供されるばかりで無く，手元に在って後の世に残される足跡進歩の記録，参考として大いに役立つことになるので大変に楽しく嬉しい事です。此の出版が世の中の認識を得て更に集団の前進として，一匹狼が集団狼として強力な力を世の中に与える事を希望します。

JAAA名誉会員
株式会社エンバイロン会長
JAF常任理事スポーツ委員長

THE RESULTS OF JAPANESE SENSE AND INGENUITY

JAAA, founded in July, 1979, has been active now for 7 years. This is the group of artists who are active in today's front line concentrating on automobiles and whose repertoire is wide. It ranges from all the land and sea vehicles to electronic equipment, cameras and other precision equipment as well as the skeletons of general leading industrial products. The artists must also wrestle with the expression of an atmosphere which is apparently labored work. Year after year the results have continued to become wonders of the industry and today they have achieved world-wide acclaim. I believe they are the fruit resulting from the subtleness and exquisite sense particularly endowed in Japanese in addition to indefatigable hard work which I would like to boast proudly to the world.

The people in this group are fellow travelers walking on the same road. At the same time, they are bitter enemies placed by fate in the same boat meaning they are competitive rivals. However, viewed from an opposite perspective, they mutually refine their skills while managing to carry on harmoniously. The growing number of members each year for this type of group may seem to be a very exceptional case.

The members were thrilled with the every-day results of the wide contribution of presentation sites from businesses and corporations who offered illustration exhibitions and various other assistance, who has highly appraised the valve of JAAA. At the same time numerous other illustrators, up-coming illustrators and those related to the publishing field have also been great influences. We would like to sincerely thank all those who made it possible to fulfill one of JAAA's goals.

This time through the courtesy of Graphic-sha Publishing, Co., Ltd., who is renowned and has a high performance record as an art publication publisher, we are very happy to introduce the full capacity of JAAA members in this gorgeous deluxe color edition specially featuring for the first time vehicles. In addition, I would like to express profound gratitude to the numerous guests who kindly cooperated with this project.

In the future we are greatly anticipating and looking forward to many young illustrators advancing into the world of industrial art. We would be more than pleased if this book can serve as a trigger to new creative ideas.

RECORDS OF STRIDES IN PROGRESS

The publishing of this deluxe edition of compiled color illustrations made possible through the efforts of all is truely an outstanding achievement. Getting together and working together at one place such as an exhibition where a display of works can be carried out has an important significance. In addition to a comprehensive survey on each individual work that and provide re-

peated pleasure, this book documents the strides in progress in a record left behind close at hand for future generations. It can also be highly useful as reference. I hope this book will gain world recognition and as a forward step towards further group organization, this book can incorporate the strength of one lone wolf into a pack to provide a mighty force in the world.

菅原　留意
Louis Sugahara

『成り立つイラスト』

近年，イラストレーターの仕事の中で，乗物のイラスト需要が急激に伸び，必然的に自動車を主とした乗物専門のイラストレーターの数も増えてきた。そして，かつて数えるほどの専門家を除き，余暇や趣味の域を出なかった乗物，とくに自動車のイラストが専門分野として成り立ってきた。これに歩調をあわせてJAAAが結成され，すでに7年になるときく。当初，同業親睦団体として発足し，相互の切磋琢磨を目的としたこの集まりが，この間に好むと好まざるとにかかわらず，多少職能団体的性格を持ってきたとしても当然である。

3年ほど前に，全メンバーの略歴・コメント・作品を一冊の本にしたが，そういう意味でこれは時期をえた出版物であった。すなわち売り手（イラストレーター）の全情報を提供することにより，買い手（クライアント）が適材を適所に依頼しうる初めてのパイプとして大きな効果があったからである。

しかし，この出版物も古くなり，かつモノクロ印刷という，時代にそぐわぬものでもあった。

たまたまグラフィック社のご好意により，今般最新の情報・作品をカラー印刷によってまとめることができた。愛好家に楽しく，クライアントへのよりアップ・ツー・デートな情報提供になると同時に，乗物イラストの歴史のひとつとしての価値もいずれ出てくるであろうことを期待している。

さて，最後にここに作品を載せられたJAAAのイラストレーター諸兄に一言申し上げたい。イラストレーターはしょせん一匹狼の職業である。親睦団体であれ職能団体であれ，ただ群がり集れば多数の力で切磋琢磨ができ，自分の職域が確保できると思ってはいけない。

一匹狼の仕事で頼れるのは自己の実力である。これが結局は自分の腕をふるう場に恵まれ，より高い評価をうる機会にもつながるのだ，ということを忘れないようにしてもらいたい。

JAAA 名誉会員
関東自動車工業株式会社　常務取締役
日本舟艇工業会　常任理事

富谷　龍一
Ryuichi Tomiya

『高度成長したイラストのレベル』

私は今年77歳になりました。カーデザイナーらしき者から，メカニズム屋と絵かきになって早何10年かになってしまった。当時デザインとは図案の一種といわれた時代であったらしく，図案家，絵かきのような者が設計室に入るのはどうだろうか，心配された様であった。昭和9年ダットサン工場での話。

考えてみれば私は天然記念物みたいな古手になってしまったものである。若かりし頃に描いたイラストを今見るとき，現在のJAAAの人達の作品から比べて，いかに貧弱なものだと思う，それだのにあの時代にあれだけ描けたのは他にいないんではないですか，と言われてなんとか慰められている。今のレベルが高くなっているのは自動車産業のレベルと同様で驚いている。

JAAA 名誉会員
富谷研究所所長

ORGANIZATION OF ILLUSTRATORS

In recent years the demand for illustrations of vehicles among all other kinds of illustrations has rapidly grown. I nevitably the number of vehicle-specializing illustrators concentrating on automobiles has increased. Thus, illustrations of vehicles, particularly cars, that did not go beyond the range of hobbies except the few specialists were organized as one of illustration field. JAAA was formed to keep in pace with this and it has already been 7 years. Starting out as a fellow worker social group, this group whose purpose was to mutually work hard together naturally took on a character of a professional association.

Three years ago brief histories, commentaries and works of all the members were compiled in one book. In a sense, this was a publication that arrived at good timing. It was, namely, highly effective as the first connecting link which by providing general information on the sellers (illustrators) the buyers (clients) could commission the right man for the right job.

However, this publication became outdated. In addition, being monochrome it became inappropriate for today.

By chance it became possible to compile them by color printing the latest up-to-date information and works through the courtesy of Graphic-sha Publishing Co., Ltd. In addition to pleasing vehicle enthusiasts and providing more up-to-date information to clients, we hope it can at the same time become valuable as a historical documentation on vehicle illustrations.

Lastly, I would like to say words to the JAAA illustrators who had their works printed in this book. The profession of an illustrator is after all a lone wolf's work. Whether JAAA is a social group or a professional group only by working hard together and combining our many strengths and resources, you should not think you can insure one's own range of work.

What can be relied on is one's own capability. This ultimately leads to that one will be given many opportunities to express one's talent and furthermore to gain higher appraisal.

THE LEVEL OF HIGH GROWTH ILLUSTRATIONS

I became 77 years old this year. Starting from work similar to car designing, I have been drawing as a mechanism specialist for many years. In those days, designs were considered as one type of drawing. Thus, I was worried about how it would be for a designer, a picture-drawing person to enter a design planning business. This occurred in the Datsun plant in 1934.

I feel I have become a veteran like a national monument. When I look at the illustrations I drew in my younger days and compare them with the present work of JAAA, mine seem somewhat meager. However, I was somewhat comforted when I was told that there was not any others in those days who drew as much as I did. I am surprised at how today's level has risen corresponding with the level of the car industry.

佃　公彦
Kimihiko Tsukuda

『クルマとマンガ』

　クルマをころがして40年になる。マンガを描きはじめてからは30年だから，差し引き10年分だけクルマ歴の方が長い。その分だけマンガよりクルマの運転の方がうまいはずである。いや確かにうまいとボクは思っている。

　クルマはどんなに長距離運転しても，苦痛に思ったことはない。マンガは2時間も机にむかっているとウンザリしてくる。クルマの運転ぐらいマンガを描くことが好きだったら，さぞかし素晴しい作品が生まれていたことだろう。

　大好きなクルマを楽しくマンガ化できたら，こんな素敵な職業はないだろうなと思うのだが，これが仕事となると地獄の責苦が待っているということになる。世の中なかなかうまくいかないものである。

　ま，できることなら，趣味の域をはみ出さない程度にクルマ漫画を描いてみようかなと，昨今考えているところである。

JAAA 名誉会員
漫画家

夏木陽介
Yosuke Natsuki

『冒険と未知が招く』

　人生には冒険とロマンが大切と，世界最過酷のパリ・ダカール・ラリーにチャレンジすること2回。そこで得た何よりの印象は，原始の地球に翻弄（ほんろう）される最新技術のメカたち，そしてその両者の間にあってこれを結ぶ人間たちのすさまじい気迫と知恵の戦い。それらはサハラに残してきたワダチが風で消えようとも，今なお砂漠の幻想とともに心のなかのワダチとして常に鮮明によみがえり，以後の人生観をすっかり変えてしまったと思っている。

　さて，私はクルマに取りつかれて30数年，

また人も知るバイク狂，本職の俳優業の殺人的スケジュールをこなしていく合間に，一人静かに絵筆をとるときの心境もまた楽しい。

　昨年のパリ・ダカのときのイラストは記念として数枚描き，今年もまたその構想を練っているものの，砂と戦った腕や指の回復を待たなければならないだろう。

　JAAAの皆さんたちも，絵のなかに冒険と未知の世界を求めて頑張って下さい。

JAAA 名誉会員
俳優

CARS AND CARTOONS

I have been driving a car for 40 years, while on the other hand, I have been drawing cartoons for 30 years which means I have 10 years more experience with cars. Therefore, this experience should afford me to be better at driving than drawing. There is no doubt, I believe, that I am a superb driver.

No matter how long or far I drive, I would never considered driving a car mental torture. However, I start to become restless after 2 hours sitting at a desk drawing. If I liked drawing cartoons as much as I did driving, imagine what fantastic work I could produce.

Also, if my favorite theme, cars, could be enjoyably made into cartoons, I do not think there would be any more ideal profession than that. However, when it comes to work, the horrors of hell would be waiting for me. Things do not come so easy in this world.

Recently, I have been considering possibilities of drawing cartoons of cars not beyond interests as a hobby.

BECKONING ADVENTURE AND THE UNKNOWN

Adventure and romance are essential spices to life. I have taken on the challenge of the world's most gruelling race, the Paris-Dakar Rally, twice. I was impressed more than anything else by the latest mechanical technology tossed at the mercy of the raw primitive earth as well as the battle of wits and the tremendous spirit of the people that bound the two forces. Although the tire tracks in the Sahara have been erased by the wind, the visions of the desert and the tire tracks imprinted in my mind are even more distinct at this moment as they constantly come back to me. Since then, my view of life has made a complete transformation.

I have been driving a car for about 30 years and as well known, I am crazy about motorcycles. Leading the murderous schedule of an actor, I sometimes enjoy, as well, the peace of mind during spare moments when I can quietly be by myself and pick up the brush and paint.

Last year I drew a few illustrations of the Paris-Dakar Rally as rememberances. I will crystallize those ideas again this year as I will probably have to wait for a recovery of my arms and fingers that fought against the sand.

I would like to tell the members of JAAA good luck and keep on pursuing the world of adventure and unknown in your pictures.

データの読み方	ACKNOWLEDGEMENT
a. 作品のタイトル	a. Title
b. 作品の発表形態	b. Published media
c. 使用した用紙及び方法	c. Paper
d. 使用した絵具等	d. Used materials
e. 原画のサイズ　単位㎜	e. Size
f. 製作年（西暦）	f. Year produced
g. クライアント名	g. Client
h. 作家氏名	h. Artist name
＊作品についてのコメント等	＊Comment on works, etc.

イラストレーション　ザ・ビークル
(ILLUSTRATED TRANSPORTATION)

Copyright © 1986
by Graphic-sha Publishing Company Ltd.
ISBN 4-7661-0382-3
Manufactured in Japan
First Edition June 1986
Graphic-sha Publishing Co., Ltd.
1-9-12 Kudan-kita Chiyoda-ku
Tokyo 102 Japan

a. 宇宙ターミナル　b. 『オムニ』アートコンテスト　c. イラストボード　d. アクリル、ガッシュ　e. 380㎜×550㎜　f. 1982年　g. 旺文社　h. 鴨下示佳　＊制作に当って細かい条件の無い、いわゆる拘束の少ないのが良かった珍しい作品。

a. SPACE TERMINAL　b. For competition　c. Illustration board　d. Acrylic and gouache　g. OBUNSHA CO., LTD.　h. Tokiyoshi Kamoshita　＊Except a few requirements or restriction, I was told to illustrate it with my style. This kind of comission was not so many.

フライト＆スペースシップ

AERIAL

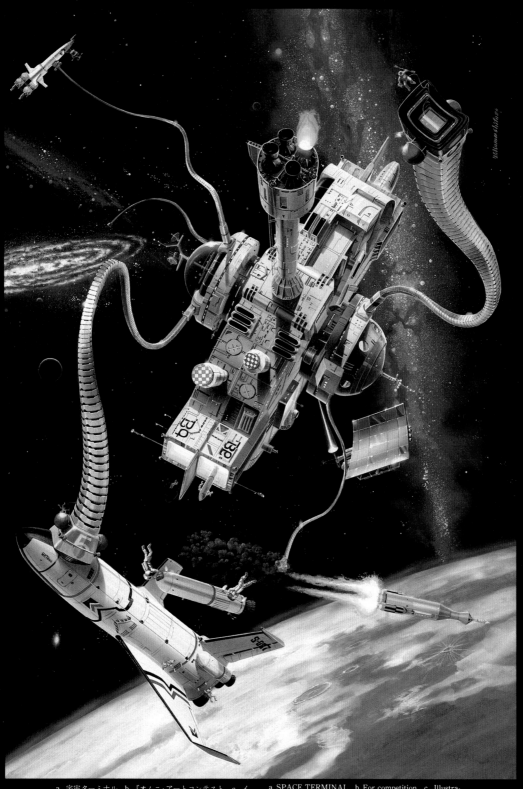

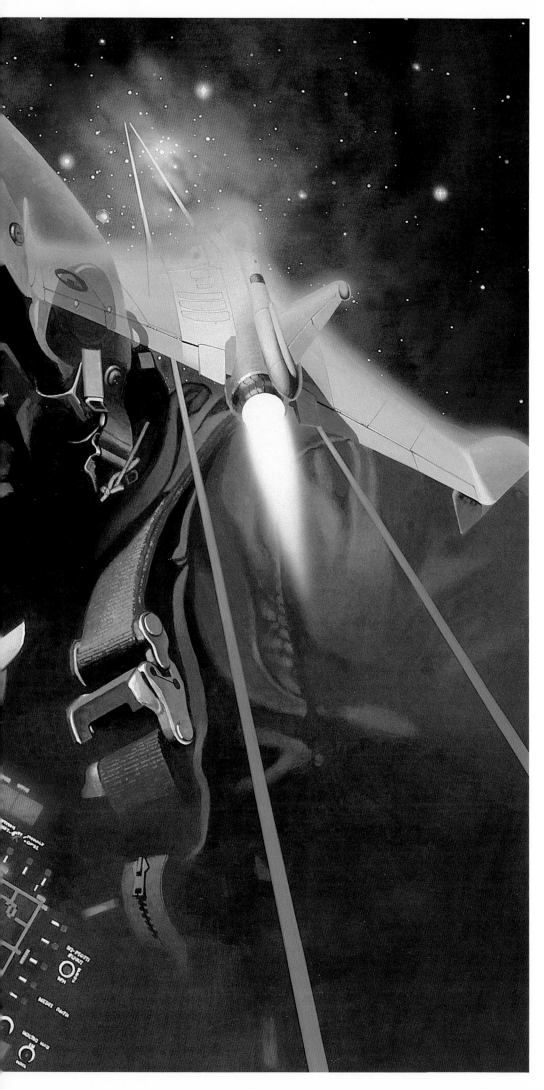

a. アルファー　スコードロン　b. パッケージ　c. ケント
紙　d. リキテックス　e. 270㍉×330㍉　f. 1984年　g.
CBS・ソニーグループ　h. 小池繁夫

a. ALPHA-SQUADRON　b. Package　c. Kent paper
d. Liquitex　g. CBS/SONY　GROUP,　INC.　h. Shigeo
Koike

IKEMATSU
753-1119

a. スーパーファイター（レーダー波吸収戦闘機）　b. 雑誌
『オムニ』　c. クレセントボード No.200　d. ガッシュ　e.
364㍉×515㍉　f. 1982年　g. 旺文社　h. 池松 均　＊
高々度である事が分かるよう空と地表との境目に苦心した。

a. SUPER JET FIGHTER　b. Magazine illustration　c.
Crescent board ＃200　d. Gouache　g. OBUNSHA CO.,
LTD.　h. Hitoshi Ikematsu　＊I tried to express the
horizon as clear as possible so that one could see the
fighter has been flying with the high altitude.

a. イー・アイ b. パッケージ c. ケント紙 d. リキテッ
クス e. 280㍉×360㍉ f. 1983年 g. CBS・ソニーグルー
プ h. 小池繁夫

a. E.I. b. Package c. Kent paper d. Liquitex g. CBS/
SONY GROUP, INC. h. Shigeo Koike

a．SFナスカのシャトル　b．書籍　c．クレセントボード
No.200　d．ガッシュ　e．424㍉×515㍉　g．旺文社　h．池
松　均　＊この時代に今と同程度の科学技術が存在したと
したらUFOに進化しているでしょう。

a. SF : SPACE SHUTTLE IN NAZCA　b. Book illustration　c. Crescent board　#200　d. Gouache　g. OBUN-
SHA CO., LTD.　h. Hitoshi Ikematsu　＊if there were a
same degree of science technology as modern times, this
shuttle would have been evolved into UFO.

a. ノースロップXB-35 フライング ウイング　b. オリジナル　c. クレセントボード No.215　d. リキテックス　e. 364㍉×515㍉　f. 1986年　h. 三五英夫　＊40年前に米国のノースロップが生涯を賭けた"夢の翼"である。SF的に画いてみた。

a. NORTHROP XB-35 FLYING WING　b. Original work　c. Crescent board #215　d. Liquitex　h. Hideo Sango　＊40 years ago, Northrop in U.S.A. developed this "Wings of Dream" as his lifework. I illustrated it with a slightly SF flavor.

a. ノースアメリカン F107　b. 航空雑誌　c. Muse KMK
ケント　d. ニッカポスターカラー他　e. 430㎜×340㎜
f. 1983年　g. エアーワールド　h. 佐竹政夫　＊モノクロ
イラストでも色が見えて来る様な絵が描けたら良いな…。

a. NORTH AMERICAN F107　b. Magazine illustration
c. kent　paper　d. Poster　color　g. AIR　WORLD　h.
Masao Satake　＊I would like to illustrate a picture that
one can feel its tint from its surface …

a. ポールスターH-01　b. オリジナル　c. NT紙　d. パ
ステル　e. 590㎜×840㎜　f. 1986年　h. 初谷秀雄　＊近
い将来，宇宙旅行を楽しめるオリジナルデザインの旅客機，
ムードに気を配った。

a. POLESTAR H-01　b. Original work　c. NT paper
d. Pastel　h. Hideo Hatsugai　＊In the near future, with
the hope that everyone can enjoy the space trip by this
original designed cruiser, I illustrated it taking care of its
atmosphere.

a. MIG-25 フォックスバット　b. 書籍　c. クレセントボ
ード　No.200　d. ガッシュ　e. 364㎜×515㎜　f. 1984年
g. 学習研究社　h. 池松　均　＊ソ連の重々しい大きな機
体を軽快に見せるため空を思い切って斜めにした。

a. MIG-25 FOXBAT　b. Book illustration　c. Crescent
board ＃200　d. Gouache　g. GAKKEN COMPANY
LTD.　h. Hitoshi・Ikematsu　＊To show the dignified
USSR planes as light as possible, I ventured on the slant
sky.

a. サーブAJ37・ビゲン　b. オリジナル　c. クレセントボ
ード　No.230　d. リキテックス　e. 364㎜×515㎜　f. 1985
年　h. 三五英夫　＊スウェーデン空軍独特のデルタ翼と迷
彩がおもしろいが，目が疲れました。

a. SAAB AJ37 VIGGEN　b. Original work　c. Crescent
board ＃230　d. Liquitex　h. Hideo Sango　＊The
delta wings and camouflaged colors of the Sweden Air
Force gave me a joy of illustration and sore eyes.

a. マグダネル・ダグラスF15イーグル　b. プラモデルパッケージ　c. ミューズKMKケント　d. ニッカポスターカラー一他　e. 305㎜×395㎜　f. 1984年　g. エルエス　h. 佐竹政夫　＊最近の飛行機はますます鳥に似て来たと思いませんか？

a. McDONNELL DOUGLAS F15 EAGLE　b. Plastic model package　c. Kent paper　d. Poster color　g. L&S CO., LTD.　h. Masao Satake　＊I have an impression that current airplanes have looked like birds gradually.

a. グラマンF14トムキャット　b. プラモデルパッケージ　c. ミューズKMKケント　d. ニッカポスターカラー一他　e. 305㎜×395㎜　f. 1984年　g. エルエス　h. 佐竹政夫　＊プラモデルの箱絵の場合，全体の形の理解しやすさが一番だと思っています。

a. GRUMMAN F-14 TOMCAT　b. Plastic model package　c. Kent paper　d. Poster color　g. L&S CO., LTD.　h. Masao Satake　＊In the case of package illustration for plastic model the most important element is understandable shape of the object.

a. F-14トムキャット　b. 図鑑　c. ケントボード　d. インク　e. 420㎜×590㎜　f. 1976年　g. 旺文社　h. 加地茂裕　＊墨入れが結構時間がかかり，カラーの方が楽です。

a. GRUMMAN F-14 TOMCAT　b. Pictorial book　c. Kent board　d. Ink　g. OBUNSHA CO., LTD.　h. Shigehiro Kaji　＊In this illustration the inking took me lots of time. For me, it's easy to use colors.

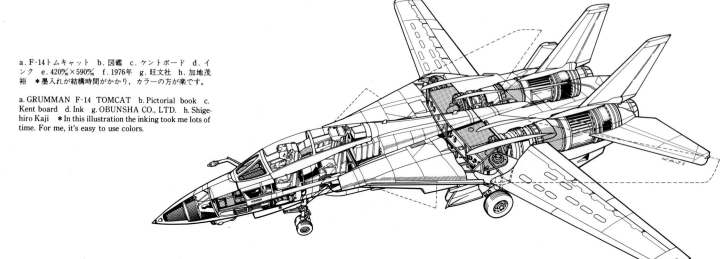

a. マクダネルダグラスF-4Gワイルド・ウィーズル　b. 雑誌表紙　c. ミューズボード B.B.ケント　d. ウィンザーニュートンガッシュ　e. 364㎜×257㎜　f. 1983年　g. TACエディション　h. 石橋謙一　＊地上から打ち上げられたSA-6ミサイルを回避中のミサイル基地攻撃用の飛行機。

a. McDONNELL DOUGLAS F-4 G WILD WEASEL
b. Magazine cover　c. Muse board BB Kent　d. Winsor Newton gouache　g. TAC EDITION　h. Ken'ichi Ishibashi　＊Basecamp-attack airplanes on evasion of SA-6 Missiles launching from the earth.

a. グラマンF-14Aトムキャット　b. 雑誌表紙　c. ミューズボード B.B.ケント　d. ウィンザーニュートンガッシュ　e. 364㎜×257㎜　f. 1984年　g. TACエディション　h. 石橋謙一　＊少し幻想的な雰囲気を出したかったので，青空でなく，赤みの強い背景にしました。

a. GRUMMAN F-14A TOMCAT　b. Magazine cover
c. Muse board BB kent　d. Winsor Newton gouache　g. TAC EDITION　h. Ken'ichi Ishibashi　＊Background is rather reddish, not blue sky, to express the surrealistic touch.

a. 輸送機のいろいろ　b. 図鑑　c. ケント紙　d. 水彩絵
具　e. 420㍉×590㍉　f. 1976年　g. 旺文社　h. 加地茂裕
＊雑誌の切り抜き資料に付細部不明。

a. VARIATION OF TRANSPORT PLANES　b. Pictorial book　c. Kent paper　d. Watercolor　g. OBUNSHA
CO., LTD.　h. Shigehiro Kaji　＊Reference photo was
cut out from a magazine. Details are rather unclear.

a. ハリアーGR-3　b. パッケージ　c. ケント紙　d. リ
キテックス　e. 220㍉×420㍉　f. 1984年　g. 長谷川製作
所　h. 小池繁夫

a. HARRIER GR MK. 3　b. Package　c. Kent paper　d.
Liquitex　g. HASEGAWA SEISAKUSHO CO., LTD.
h. Shigeo Koike

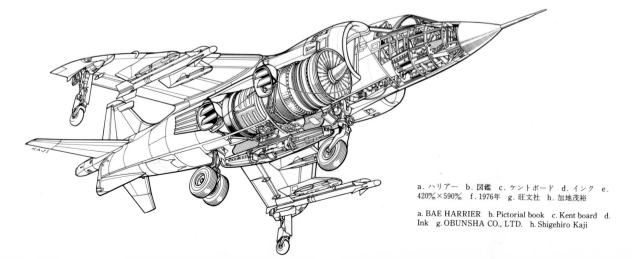

a. ハリアー　b. 図鑑　c. ケントボード　d. インク　e.
420㍉×590㍉　f. 1976年　g. 旺文社　h. 加地茂裕

a. BAE HARRIER　b. Pictorial book　c. Kent board　d.
Ink　g. OBUNSHA CO., LTD.　h. Shigehiro Kaji

a. サンダーバーズ　b. オリジナル　c. クレセントボード
No.310　d. リキテックス　e. 364㍉×515㍉　f. 1984年
h. 相川修一

a. THUNDERBIRDS　b. Original work　c. Crescent
board #310　d. Liquitex　h. Shuichi Aikawa

a. 三菱T-2　b. パッケージ　c. ケント紙　d. リキテッ
クス　e. 220㍉×420㍉　f. 1985年　g. 長谷川製作所　h.
小池繁夫

a. MITSUBISHI T-2　b. Package　c. Kent paper　d.
Liquitex　g. HASEGAWA SEISAKUSHO CO., LTD.
h. Shigeo Koike

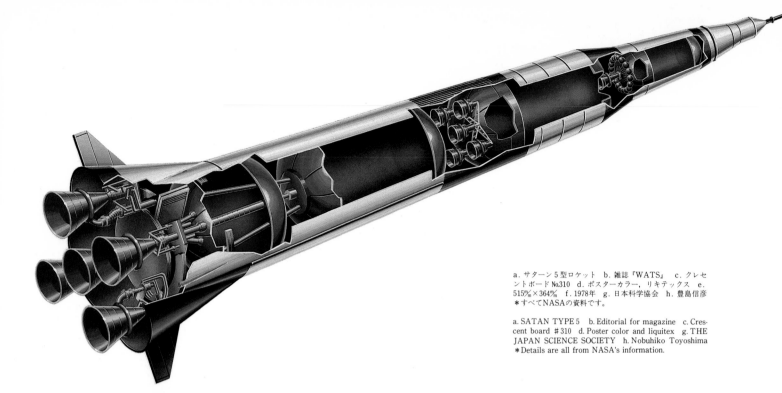

a. サターン5型ロケット　b. 雑誌『WATS』　c. クレセ
ントボード No.310　d. ポスターカラー，リキテックス　e.
515㎜×364㎜　f. 1978年　g. 日本科学協会　h. 豊島信彦
＊すべてNASAの資料です。

a. SATAN TYPE 5　b. Editorial for magazine　c. Cres-
cent board ＃310　d. Poster color and liquitex　g. THE
JAPAN SCIENCE SOCIETY　h. Nobuhiko Toyoshima
＊Details are all from NASA's information.

a. 宇宙基地建設　b. 『世界日報』誌上　c. ケント紙　d.
ポスターカラー，墨汁　e. 250㎜×250㎜　f. 1985年　g.
世界日報社　h. 出射忠明　＊宇宙時代への夢の第一歩とし
て宇宙基地の初歩的なものの建設風景を表現した。

a. CONSTRUCTION OF THE SPACE CAMP b.
Editorial for daily newspaper　c. Kent paper　d. Poster
color and Indian ink　g. THE SEKAI NIPPO　h. Tadaaki Idei　＊Construction scene of the elementary space
camp is illustrated to express the first step toward the
space era.

a. 宇宙ステーション　b. 新聞広告　c. クレセントボード
d. リキテックス　e. 230㍉×250㍉　f. 1979年　g. 松下電
器産業　h. 武田育雄

a. THE SPACE STATION b. Ad for newspaper c.
Crescent board d. Liquitex g. MATSUSHITA
ELECTRIC INDUSTRIAL CO., LTD. h. Ikuo Takeda

a．パイロット　b．オリジナル　c．クレセントボード
№310　d．リキテックス　e．515㎜×364㎜　f．1984年
h．相川修一

a. PILOT　b. Original work　c. Crescent board ＃310
d. Liquitex　h. Shuichi Aikawa

a．シュミレーション・ゲーム　b．雑誌さし絵　c．クレセ
ントボード№310　d．鉛筆，リキテックス，ガッシュ　e．
315㎜×380㎜　f．1983年　g．アスキー出版　h．佐原輝夫
＊コンピュータゲーム記事のさし絵。戦略上の要素をすべ
て盛り込むのが目的。

a. SIMULATION GAME　b. Editorial for magazine　c.
Crescent board ＃310　d. Liquitex and gouache　g.
ASCII PUBLISHING CO.　h. Telly Sahara　＊This
work was used for the editorial column on computer
game, purposed to include all the elements on strategies.

a. ハインケルHe177グライフ b. 未発表 c. ミューズボードB.B.ケント(細目) d. ウィンザーニュートンガッシュ e. 515㎜×728㎜ f. 1984年 g. 岡田 豊 h. 石橋謙一 ＊第2次大戦中にドイツで作られた野心的な爆撃機で、大西洋上で船団攻撃中である。

a. HEINKEL HE177 GREIF b. Private collection c. Muse board BB kent d. Winsor Newton gouache g. MR. YUTAKA OKADA h. Kenichi Ishibashi ＊A bomber made in Germany during the W.W. II is attacking a fleet of vessels on the Atlantic Ocean.

a. 試作機キ-87 b. オリジナル c. イラストボード d. ポスターカラー e. 270㎜×395㎜ f. 1986年 h. 出射忠明 ＊少年時代に関係した思い出の機。側面にあるのはターボチャージャー。下は試作工場。

a. EXPERIMENT KI-87 b. Original work c. Illustration board d. Poster color h. Tadaaki Idei ＊This plane reminds me of my boyhood. The side attached is turbo charger and below seen is its factory.

a. ボーイングB-17フライングフォートレス b. 雑誌 c. イラストボード d. 水彩絵具 e. 420㎜×590㎜ f. 1980年 g. 文林堂 h. 加地茂裕 ＊資料写真が小さく暗いので細部が不明、かなりインチキな絵になってしまった。

a. BOEING B-17 FLYING FORTRESS b. Magazine illustration c. Kent board d. Watercolor g. BUNRIN-DO CO., LTD. h. Shigehiro Kaji ＊As the reference photo was so small, dark, and unclear in detail that this work was rather fake, I was afraid.

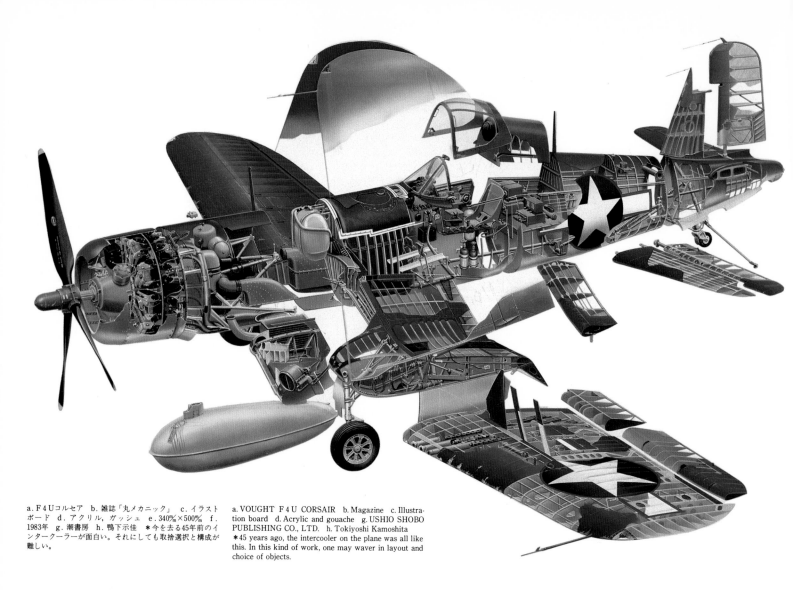

a. F4Uコルセア　b. 雑誌「丸メカニック」　c. イラスト
ボード　d. アクリル, ガッシュ　e. 340㍉×500㍉　f.
1983年　g. 潮書房　h. 鴨下示佳　＊今を去る45年前のイ
ンタークーラーが面白い。それにしても取捨選択と構成が
難しい。

a. VOUGHT F4U CORSAIR　b. Magazine　c. Illustration board　d. Acrylic and gouache　g. USHIO SHOBO
PUBLISHING CO., LTD.　h. Tokiyoshi Kamoshita
＊45 years ago, the intercooler on the plane was all like
this. In this kind of work, one may waver in layout and
choice of objects.

a. RAF第一中隊　b. 雑誌口絵　c. クレセンドボード
№99　d. リキテックス　e. 287㍉×348㍉　f. 1980年　g.
双葉社　h. 穂積和夫　＊1918年の歴史的な写真をもとに描
いた作品。

a. PILOTS OF R.A.F. SQUARDRON №1　b. Editorial
for magazine　c. Crescent board ＃99　d. Liquitex　g.
FUTABASHA CO., LTD.　h. Kazuo Hozumi　＊This
illustration was based on the historical photograph in
1918.

a. 紫電改のコクピット　b. 雑誌　c. ケント紙　d. アク
リル　e. 380㍉×540㍉　f. 1979年　g. 潮書房　h. 高荷義
之

a. COCKPIT　b. Magazine illustration　c. Kent paper
d. Acrylic　g. USHIO SHOBO PUBLISHING CO., LTD.
h. Yoshiyuki Takani

a. 93式双発軽爆撃機　b. カレンダー　c. ケント紙　d. リ
キテックス　e. 315㍉×400㍉　f. 1985年　g. 富士重工業
h. 小池繁夫

a. TYPE 93 TWIN-ENGINED LIGHT-BOMBER b.
Calendar c. Kent paper d. Liquitex g. FUJI HEAVY

a. 日本航空機製造 YS-11　b. ボックス・アート　c. B.B.
ケント　d. ウィンザーニュートンガッシュ　e. 364㍉×
515㍉　f. 1983年　g. バンダイ　h. 石橋謙一　＊戦後日
本で初めて開発された輸送機です。輸送，救難に現在も活躍
中です。

a. NAMC YS-11　b. Package illustration　c. BB kent
d. Winsor Newton gouache　g. BANDAI CO., LTD. h.
Ken'ichi Ishibashi ＊ The first transport plane
developed in Japan after the W.W. II. It has been, and
still is active in a transporation and a rescue.

a. ポール・マンツ　b. 雑誌口絵　c. クレセントボード
No.99　d. リキテックス　e. 362㍉×436㍉　f. 1980年　g.
婦人画報社　h. 穂積和夫　＊シネラマ撮影に活躍するハリ
ウッドの航空カメラマン，ポール・マンツ。

a. PAUL MANTZ b. Editorial for magazine c. Crescent board ＃99 d. Liquitex g. THE FUJIN GAHO-
SHA h. Kazuo Hozumi ＊Aerial photographer, Paul
Manz who had been active in taking Cinerama, was
flying over pyramids.

a. ロッキード "シリウス"　b. カレンダー　c. ケント紙
d. リキテックス　e. 315㎜×400㎜　f. 1985年　g. 富士重
工業　h. 小池繁夫

a. LOCKHEEDS "SIRIUS"　b. Calendar　c. Kent paper
d. Liquitex　g. FUJI HEAVY INDUSTRIES LTD.　h.
Shigeo Koike

a. 空中戦　b. オリジナル　c. クレセントボード No.310
d. ホルベインカラーインク, リキテックス　e. 350㎜×
260㎜　f. 1985年　h. 安田雅章　＊ヨーロッパの深い森の
雰囲気を出すのに苦労した。

a. AERIAL WAR　b. Original work　c. Crescent board
#310　d. Drawing ink and liquitex　h. Masaaki Yasuda
＊I did it with much efforts to capture the deep forest
colors of Europe.

a. ナンジェッセの着陸　b. 雑誌口絵　c. キャンバス　d.
リキテックス　e. 517㎜×640㎜　f. 1973年　g. 婦人画報
社　h. 穂積和夫　＊第1次大戦当時のエピソードを描いた
連作のひとつ。

a. THE LANDING OF CHARLES NUNGESSER　b.
Editorial for magazine　c. Canvas　d. Liquitex　g. THE
FUJIN GAHOSHA　h. Kazuo Hozumi　＊One of serial
works drawn a episode during the W.W.I.

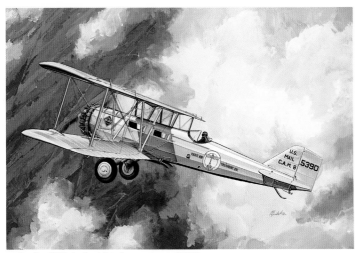

a. ボーイング40B-4　b. オリジナル　c. ミューズKMK
ケント　d. ニッカポスターカラー他　e. 455㎜×605㎜
f. 1975年　h. 佐竹政夫　＊この時代のヒコーキは人間く
さくて良いのですね。

a. BOEING 40 B-4　b. Original work　c. Kent paper　d
. Poster color and mixed media　h. Masao Satake
＊Don't you think an airplane of these times looks
human ?

a. 川崎ヒューズ OH-6D　b. ボックス・アート　c. ミュ
ーズボードB.B.ケント　d. ウィンザーニュートンガッシュ
e. 364㎜×515㎜　f. 1982年　g. フジミ模型　h. 石橋謙一
＊富士演習場で戦車隊の支援に当たるOH-6D。

a. KAWASAKI HUGHES OH-6D　b. Package illustration　c. Muse board BB kent　d. Winsor Newton gouache　g. FUJIMI MOKEI CO., LTD.　h. Ken'ichi Ishibashi
＊OH-6D supporting a tank corps in Fuji Maneuvers.

a. 米軍ヘリ HH-1H　b. オリジナル　c. キャンバスボ
ード　d. リキテックス　e. 400㎜×510㎜　f. 1986年　h.
中村 信

a. UNITED STATES ARMY HH-1H　b. Original
work　c. Canvas board　d. Liquitex　h. Shin Nakamura

a. 帆船カティサーク　b. 商品のボックスアート　c. ワトソンボート　d. ポスターカラー, ガッシュ　e. 515㎜× 725㎜　f. 1977年　g. 今井科学　h. 上田毅八郎　＊海のロマンを絵筆に託してインド洋を快走中のカティサーク号併走中の僚船より見る。

a. SAILING SHIP CUTTY SARK　b. Package illustration　c. Watson board　d. Poster color and gouache　g. IMAI KAGAKU CO., LTD.　h. Kihachiro Ueda　＊The Cutty Sark Sailing on the Indian Ocean. View from the colleague vessels aside.

シップ

SHIPS

a. 帆船（日本丸）　b. ポスター　c. B.B.ケント　d. リキ
テックス他　e. 515㍉×728㍉　f. 1959年　g. 埼玉銀行
h. 野上隼夫　＊日本丸建造が始まった頃に描いたため，資
料不足で大変でした。

a. THE NIPPON MARU　b. Poster　c. Kent paper　d.
Liquitex　g. SAITAMA BANK LTD.　h. Hayao Isao
＊Short of references annoyed me as I illustrated it
during the days her construction had started.

a. 帆船（日本丸）　b. ポスター　c. B.B.ケント　d. リキ
テックス他　e. 728㍉×515㍉　f. 1959年　g. 埼玉銀行
h. 野上隼夫　＊逆光で帆を透かして見える感じを表した。

a. THE NIPPON MARU　b. Poster　c. Kent paper　d.
Liquitex　g. SAITAMA BANK LTD.　h. Hayao
Nogami　＊I tried to illustrate an atmosphere of her
transparent sails backlighted.

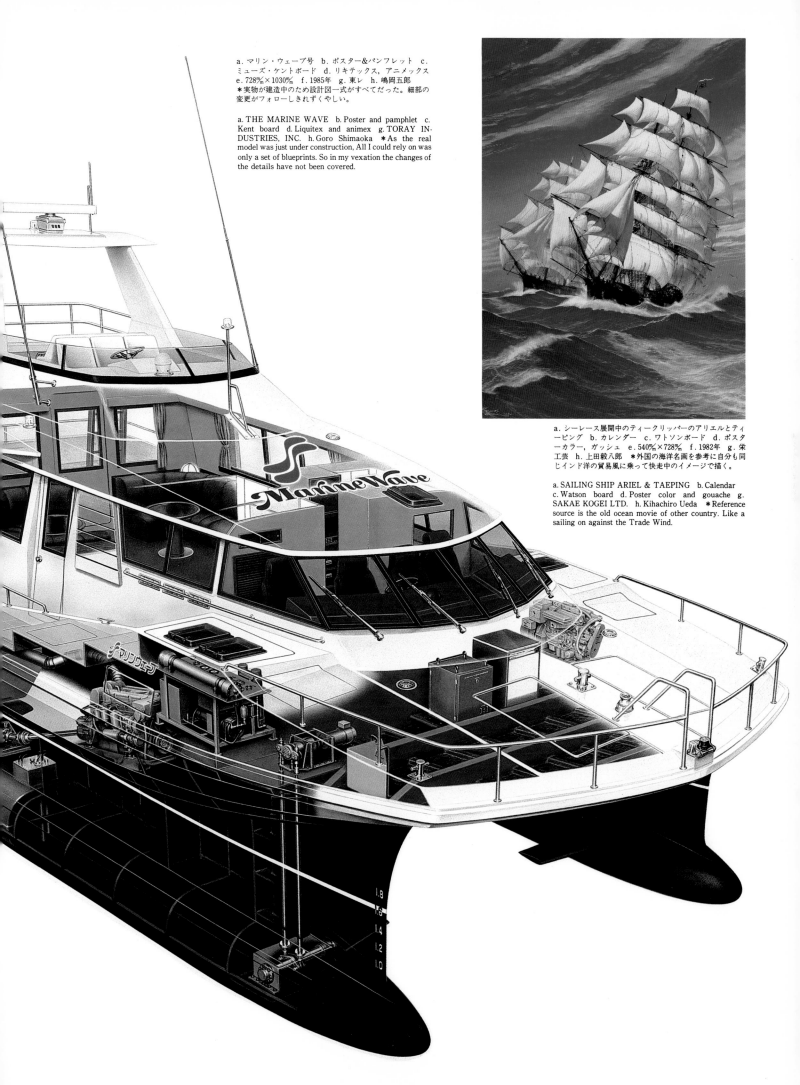

a. マリン・ウェーブ号　b. ポスター＆パンフレット　c.
ミューズ・ケントボード　d. リキテックス，アニメックス
e. 728㍉×1030㍉　f. 1985年　g. 東レ　h. 嶋岡五郎
＊実物が建造中のため設計図一式がすべてだった。細部の
変更がフォローしきれずくやしい。

a. THE MARINE WAVE　b. Poster and pamphlet　c.
Kent board　d. Liquitex and animex　g. TORAY IN-
DUSTRIES, INC.　h. Goro Shimaoka　＊As the real
model was just under construction, All I could rely on was
only a set of blueprints. So in my vexation the changes of
the details have not been covered.

a. シーレース展開中のティークリッパーのアリエルとティ
ーピング　b. カレンダー　c. ワトソンボード　d. ポスタ
ーカラー，ガッシュ　e. 540㍉×728㍉　f. 1982年　g. 栄
工芸　h. 上田毅八郎　＊外国の海洋名画を参考に自分も同
じインド洋の貿易風に乗って快走中のイメージで描く。

a. SAILING SHIP ARIEL & TAEPING　b. Calendar
c. Watson board　d. Poster color and gouache　g.
SAKAE KOGEI LTD.　h. Kihachiro Ueda　＊Reference
source is the old ocean movie of other country. Like a
sailing on against the Trade Wind.

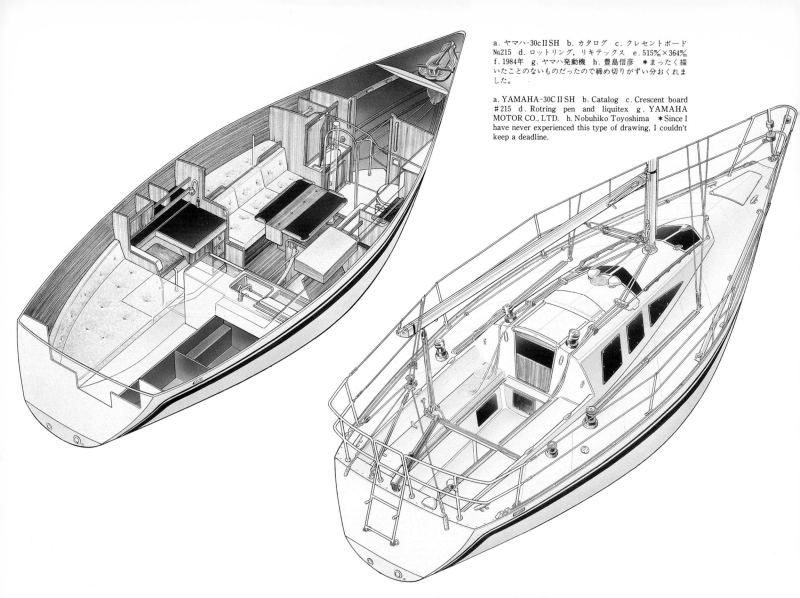

a. ヤマハ-30cⅡSH　b. カタログ　c. クレセントボード
No.215　d. ロットリング, リキテックス　e. 515㎜×364㎜
f. 1984年　g. ヤマハ発動機　h. 豊島信彦　＊まったく描
いたことのないものだったので締め切りがずい分おくれま
した。

a. YAMAHA-30CⅡSH　b. Catalog　c. Crescent board
#215　d. Rotring pen and liquitex　g. YAMAHA
MOTOR CO., LTD.　h. Nobuhiko Toyoshima　＊Since I
have never experienced this type of drawing, I couldn't
keep a deadline.

a. 風　b. オリジナル　c. クレセントボード No.115　d. リ
キテックス　e. 200㎜×310㎜　f. 1985年　h. 中村 信
＊風に向かっている感じが出したかった。船は想像なので
現実には無い。

a. AGAINST THE WIND　b. Original work　c. Crescent board #115　d. Liquitex　h. Shin Nakamura　＊I
tried to feature the thrilling feeling of the sail on against
the wind. This ship has no real model in particular.

a. サイプレス b. オリジナル c. NT紙 d. パステル他
e. 590㎜×840㎜ f. 1986年 h. 初谷秀雄 ＊直線を生か
した約10人乗りのオリジナルデザインのクルーザー。

a. CYPRESS b. Original work c. NT paper d. Pastel
and others h. Hideo Hatsugai ＊Nearly ten-seaters
cruiser is made the best use of beautiful straight lines.
Original design.

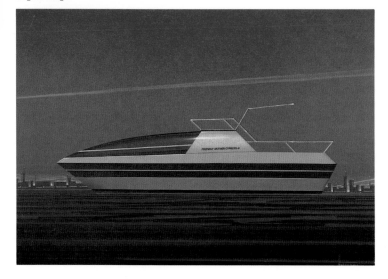

a. 波力発電実験船 b. 九州電力「電力館」 c. クレセント
ボード d. ガッシュ e. 364㎜×515㎜ f. 1984年 g. 海
洋科学技術センター h. 池松 均 ＊新設計のタービン室
のしくみ中心に表現，資料は現場取材中心です。

a. WAVE-POWER GENERATOR b. Exhibited work
c. Crescent board ♯200 d. Gouache g. JAPAN MAR-
INE SCIENCE AND TECHNOLOGY CENTER h.
Hitoshi Ikematsu ＊Mainly represented the system of
the newly designed turbin room. I myself went to see the
real model for the investigation.

a. 南極観測船しらせ b. 教育雑誌 c. クレセントボード
№200 d. ガッシュ e. 364㎜×515㎜ f. 1985年 g. 小
学館 h. 池松 均 ＊この手のものは全体が硬くなりやす
いので南極ペンギンとヘリで調子に変化をあたえた。

a. SHIRASE b. Magazine illustration c. Crescent
board ♯200 d. Gouache g. SHOGAKUKAN h. Hitoshi Ikematsu ＊This type of illustration is inclined to be
rather hard-touched. To avoid it, I gave some variations
on it with Antarctic penguins and helicopters.

a. 香取丸　b. カレンダー　c. B.B.ケント　d. リキテック
ス他　e. 364㍉×515㍉　f. 1959年　g. 日本郵船　h. 野上
隼夫　＊逆光追風の中を航行しているシーンを描いた。

a. THE KATORI MARU　b. Calendar　c. Kent paper
d. Liquitex　g. NIPPON YUSEN KAISHA　h. Hayao
Nogami　＊Scene of her sailing on against the wind and
light.

a. 浅間丸　b. カレンダー　c. B.B.ケント　d. リキテック
ス他　e. 364㍉×515㍉　f. 1959年　g. 日本郵船　h. 野上
隼夫　＊戦前の日本客船を代表する船の一つです。

a. THE ASAMA MARU　b. Calendar　c. Kent paper
d. Liquitex　g. NIPPON YUSEN KAISHA　h. Hayao
Nogami　＊This is one of the representative liners in
Japan before W.W.II.

a. レイズ ザ タイタニック　b. 映画ポスター　c. クレセントボード No.115　d. リキテックス　e. 1030㎜×750㎜　f. 1982年　g. 東宝東和　h. 中村　信　＊映画の中にもこの場面はなく、すべて想像で描いたもの。船は映画のスチール写真を参考にした。

a. RAISE THE TITANIC　b. Movie poster　c. Crescent board #115　d. Liquitex　g. TOHO-TOWA COMPANY LTD.　h. Shin Nakamura　＊Originally this situation was not illustrated in the movie. It means I have drawn it completely from my imagination. The Taitanic was sourced from the movie stills.

a. イタリア客船ラ・ファエロ　b. オリジナル　c. ワトソンボード　d. ポスターカラー、透明水彩　e. 500㎜×728㎜　f. 1977年　h. 上田穀八郎　＊船は舵より見るのが一番美しい。ある船の雑誌より良い写真があったので習作として描く。

a. ITALIAN LINER RAFFAELO　b. Original work　c. Watson board　d. Poster color and watercolor　h. Kihachiro Ueda　＊A view from the stern is the most beautiful, I believe. I illustrated it for my exercise when I find a good reference in a ship magazine.

a. 日本海軍航空母艦「大鳳」 b. オリジナル c. ワトソンボード d. ガッシュ，透明水彩 e. 418㍉×530㍉ f. 1982年 h. 上田毅八郎 ＊戦争の体験を生かし太平洋の荒海を同行中の僚艦より見た姿を描いてみた。

a. JAPAN AIRCRAFT CARRIER TAIHO b. Original work c. Watson board d. Gouache and watercolor h. Kihachiro Ueda ＊This was illustrated through my war-experiences.

a. キーパーズ オブ ザ シー b. オリジナル c. クレセントボード No.100 d. リキテックス e. 250㍉×400㍉ f. 1986年 h. 大内 誠 ＊昔，アメリカの模型のパッケージイラストに良い物が多かった。確か，こんなのもあった。

a. KEEPERS OF THE SEA b. Original work c. Crescent board ＃100 d. Liquitex h. Makoto Ouchi ＊I met many good examples of package illustrations for the plastic models made in America. This is the one I remembered among them.

a. ミッドウェイ海戦　b. パッケージ　c. イラストボード　a. OPERATION "MI"　b. Package illustration　c. Illus-
d. アクリル　e. 300㍉×400㍉　f. 1984年　g. ツクダホビ　tration board　d. Acrylic　g. TSUKUDA HOBBY CO.,
ー　h. 高荷義之　LTD.　h. Yoshiyuki Takani

a. 第一次ソロモン海戦の鳥海　b. 展覧会用　c. イラスト
ボード　d. ガッシュ，アクリル　e. 400㎜×750㎜　f. 不
明　h. 鴨下示佳　＊1942年8月8日の「鳥海」を史実に忠
実なシーンを再現しようと念じて仕上げましたが……。

a. THE CHOKAI b. Exhibited work c. Illustration
board d. Gouache and acrylic h. Tokiyoshi Kamoshita
＊I have tried to reproduce this great warship, the Chokai, carefully and precisely on the historical references.

a. 新8・8艦隊　b. 新聞紙面　c. トレーシングペーパー
d. 墨汁，丸ペン，ロットリング　e. 260㎜×364㎜　f. 1985
年　g. 大阪新聞社　h. 出射忠明　＊海上自衛隊のヘリ8
機と護衛艦8隻による新編成。旧海軍の八・八艦隊の名称を
受けついだ。

a. THE NEW 8．8 FLEETER b. Editorial for newspaper c. Tracing paper d. Indian ink, pen, rotling pen
g. OSAKA SINBUN h. Tadaaki Idei ＊8 helicopters of
the Maritime Self-Defence Force and 8 guard warships
were named The New 8.8. Fleeter after the naval's.

a. 南太平洋海戦　b. パッケージ　c. イラストボード　d.
アクリル　e. 295㎜×460㎜　f. 1985年　g. ツクダホビー
h. 高荷義之

a. THE BATTLE OF SANTA CRUZ　b. Package illustration　c. Illustration board　d. Acrylic　g. TSUKUDA HOBBY CO., LTD.　h. Yoshiyuki Takani

a. 眼下の敵　b. パッケージ　c. イラストボード　d. ア
クリル　e. 360㎜×510㎜　f. 1984年　g. ツクダホビー
h. 高荷義之

a. EMEMY BELOW　b. Package illustration　c. Illustration board　d. Acrylic　g. TSUKUDA HOBBY CO., LTD.　h. Yoshiyuki Takani

カー
＆
ドライバー

CARS & DRIVERS

a．コルベット・スティングレイ　b．雑誌表紙　c．クレセントボード No.215　d．リキテックス　e．365㍉×420㍉　f．1984年　g．ダイヤモンド社　h．岡本三紀夫　＊スタジオで撮影した車だったので外の風景に合わせるのに色，その他で苦労しました。

a. CORVETTE STINGRAY b. Magazine cover c. Crescent board ＃215 d. Liquitex g. DIAMOND, INC. h. Mikio Okamoto ＊Reference photo was taken inside studio, so I had to illustrate additional surroundings from my own imagination.

a. フェアレディ Mr.1　b. 雑誌表紙　c. コンピュータ・グ
ラフィックス　f. 1985年　g. 内外出版社　h. 岡本　博

a. FAIR LADY MR.1　b. Magazine cover　c. Computer
graphics　g. NAIGAI SHUPPANSHA　h. Hiroshi
Okamoto

a. フェラーリ・テスタロッサ　b. オリジナル　c. ヴィン
セント・ヴェラム　d. マジック・マーカー, プリスマパス
テル他　e. 350㎜×430㎜　f. 1986年　h. 児玉英雄

a. FERRARI TESTAROSSA　b. Original work　c. Vellum paper　d. Marker and pastel　h. Hideo Kodama

CATERHAM CAR SALES

a. ケイターハム スーパー7　b. オリジナル　c. オリオンプロフェッショナルボード　d. リキテックス　e. 312㍉×290㍉　f. 1983年　h. 榎本竹利　＊数年前1人でブラリと出掛けたヨーロッパ自動車見聞旅行。ケイターハムでの思い出です。

a. CATERHAM SUPER 7　b. Original work　c. Orion professional board　d. Liquitex　h. Taketoshi Enomoto　＊A few years ago I traveled to Europe by myself to see cars. This is the reminiscence of Caterham.

a. シボレーコルベット　b. カレンダー　c. フォトコピー
d. パントンカラーオーバーレイ　e. 275㎜×350㎜　f.
1984年　g. タカラ　h. 中村安広

a. CHEVROLET　CORVETTE　b. Calendar　c. Photo
copy　d. Pantone color overlay　g. TAKARA CO., LTD.
h. Yasuhiro Nakamura

a. ホンダ　インテグラ　b. オリジナル　c. ハレパネ　d.
リキテックス, ロットリング　e. 350㎜×500㎜　f. 1985年
h. 稲垣謙治

a. HONDA　INTEGRA　b. Original　work　c. Panel　d.
Liquitex and rotring pen　h. Kenji Inagaki

a．ホンダS800 b．雑誌表紙 c．コンピュータ・グラフィ
ックス f．1985年 g．内外出版社 h．岡本 博

a. HONDA S800 b. Magazine cover c. Computer graphics g. NAIGAI SHUPPANSHA h. Hiroshi Okamoto

a．BMWイセッタ b．雑誌の表紙 c．キャンソン紙 d．
ドローイング・インキ e．257㎜×364㎜ f．1985年 g．
リクルート h．永野清貴 ＊こんな車もいいですネ。

a. BMW ISETTA b. Magazine cover c. Canson paper
d. Drawing ink e. 257㎜×364㎜ f. 1985年 g. RECRUIT CO., LTD. h. Kiyotaka
Nagano ＊Nice car, isn't it.

a. コルベット 1982 b. 雑誌の表紙 c. キャンソン紙 d.
ドローイング・インキ e. 257㎜×364㎜ f. 1986年 g.
リクルート h. 永野清貴 ＊ウーム，きまっている。

a. CORVETTE 1982 b. Magazine cover c. Canson
paper d. Drawing ink g. RECRUIT CO., LTD. h.
Kiyotaka Nagano ＊h'm... Looks dandy.

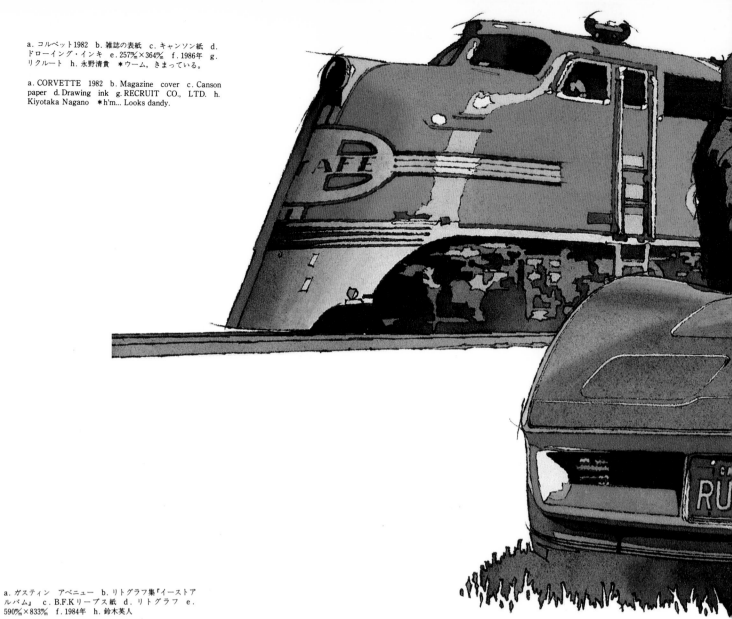

a. ガスティン アベニュー b. リトグラフ集『イーストア
ルバム』 c. B.F.K リーブス紙 d. リトグラフ e.
590㎜×833㎜ f. 1984年 h. 鈴木英人

a. GUSTINE AVE. b. Portfolio c. B.F.K. Leaves paper
d. Lithograph h. Eizin Suzuki

a．フェラーリ365GTC　b．雑誌　c．クレセントボード
№215　d．リキテックス　e．365㎜×420㎜　f．1984年
g．ダイヤモンド社　h．岡本三紀夫　＊紺のボディのため、
黒い色に見えない様に注意しました。

a. FERRARI 365 GTC　b. Magazine illustration　c. Crescent board ＃215　d. Liquitex　g. DIAMOND, INC.　h.
Mikio Okamoto　＊Point was navy-blue body... It must
be absolutely in deep blue, but not in black.

a. フォルクスワーゲン　b. 雑誌表紙　c. クレセントボード　№215　d. リキテックス　e. 365㎜×420㎜　f. 1984年　g. ダイヤモンド社　h. 岡本三紀夫　＊いつもそうなのですが、バックと車の関係、影のつき方など何枚もの資料を集めました。

a. VW　b. Magazine cover　c. Crescent board #215　d. Liquitex　g. DIAMOND, INC.　h. Mikio Okamoto　＊I have collected as many references as possible, to check the relations of background and a car itself, or shadows. This is my usual way of working.

a. ホテル　カーライル　b. イラスト集『アメリカンロードショウ』　c. KMKケント紙　d. ロットリング, パントーン・オーバーレイ　e. 364㎜×517㎜　f. 1985年　g. 東宝　h. 鈴木英人

a. HOTEL CARLYLE　b. Portfolio　c. Kent paper　d. Rotring pen and pantone color overlay　g. TOHO CO., LTD.　h. Eizin Suzuki

a. フェラーリ275GTS b. 雑誌表紙 c. クレセントボー
ド No.215 d. リキテックス e. 365㎜×420㎜ f. 1984年
g. ダイヤモンド社 h. 岡本三紀夫 ＊赤いボディは印刷
の時ベターッとした調子になるので原画はかなりコントラ
ストをつけています。

a. FERRARI 275 GTS b. Magazine cover c. Crescent
board #215 d. Liquitex g. DIAMOND, INC. h. Mikio
Okamoto ＊Sometime the red body is printed in flat-
touched. So I illustrated its original in the high-contrast-
ed touches.

a. フェラーリ250GT b. オリジナル c. クレセントボー
ド No.300 d. リキテックス e. 364㎜×515㎜ f. 1983年
h. 森 優 ＊個展に展示するために描いたイラストレーシ
ョン，ザ・グレイティスト・カーを参考。

a. FERRARI 250 GT b. Original work c. Crescent
board #300 d. Liquitex h. Yu Mori ＊To exhibite in
my one-man show. Source is also "The Greatest Car".

a. ジャギュア　タイプ　ル・マン　b. 雑誌表紙　c. コンピュータ・グラフィックス　f. 1985年　g. 内外出版社　h. 岡本　博

a. JAGUAR TYPE LE MANN　b. Magazine cover　c. Computer graphics　g. NAIGAI SHUPPANSHA　h. Hiroshi Okamoto

a. ギャランΣ　b. ポスター　c. クレセントボード No.310　d. リキテックス，ガッシュ　e. 430㎜×600㎜　f. 1985年　g. 三菱自動車　h. 佐原輝夫　＊TVCFと連動するため，人物の配置，動き，表情等に気を配った。

a. GALANT Σ　b. Poster　c. Crescent board ＃310　d. Liquitex and gouache　g. MITSUBISHI MOTOR CO., LTD.　h. Telly Sahara　＊As this work has been produced in the purpose of collaboration with TVCF, I did it very carefully, especially with the position, movement, and expression of the galleries.

a. メルセデスベンツ450SL　b. 雑誌『カー＆ドライバー』
c. キャンバスボード　d. リキテックス　e. 530㎜×450㎜
f. 1983年　g. ダイヤモンド社　h. 小森　誠

a. MERCEDES-BENZ 450SL　b. Magazine illustration
c. Canvas board　d. Liquitex　g. DIAMOND, INC.　h.
Makoto Komori

a. ポルシェ911ターボ　b. カレンダー　c. フォトコピー
d. パントンカラーオーバーレイ　e. 275㎜×350㎜　f.
1984年　g. タカラ　h. 中村安広

a. PORSCHE 911 TURBO　b. Calendar　c. Photo copy
d. Pantone color overlay　g. TAKARA CO., LTD.　h.
Yasuhiro Nakamura

a. ポルシェ356　b. 雑誌　c. イラストボード　d. アクリ
ル絵具　e. 320㎜×360㎜　f. 1984年　g. ダイヤモンド社
h. 井川友晴

a. PORSCHE 356　b. Magazine cover　c. Illustration
board　d. Acrylic　g. DIAMOND, INC.　h. Tomoharu
Ikawa

a. スバル360　b. 自動車雑誌　c. ケント紙　d. ペン＆イ
ンク　e. 295㍉×245㍉　f. 1983年　g. 八重州出版　h. 榎
本竹利

a. SUBARU 360　b. Magazine illustration　c. Kent paper
d. Pen & ink　g. YAESU PUBLISHING CO., LTD.　h.
Taketoshi Enomoto

a. プリムス　フューリー　b. 雑誌表紙　c. クレセントボ
ード №215　d. リキテックス　e. 365㍉×420㍉　f. 1984
年　g. ダイヤモンド社　h. 岡本三紀夫　＊この当時のア
メリカの車はかなり大きく人物との対比が大変難しいもの
です。

a. PLYMOUTH FURY　b. Magazine cover　c. Crescent
board #215　d. Liquitex　g. DIAMOND, INC.　h. Mikio
Okamoto　＊American cars in these days were rather
large-typed. So the contrast with the car and a man was
very difficult.

a. A型フォードホットロッド　b. 雑誌『カー＆ドライバー』
c. キャンバスボード　d. リキテックス　e. 530㎜×450㎜
f. 1983年　g. ダイヤモンド社　h. 小森　誠

a. TYPE A, FORD HOTROD　b. Magazine illustration
c. Canvas board　d. Liquitex　g. DIAMOND, INC.　h.
Makoto Komori

a. セリカ 1978年型　b. 自動車専門誌新車予想企画　c. イラストボード　d. ガッシュ　e. 500㍉×700㍉　f. 1977年　g. 八重州出版　h. 小谷智昭　＊発表前の新車を予想して描くので、情報分析に手間がかかった。適中率は95％と思う。

a. TOYOTA CELICA '78　b. Editorial for magazine　c. Illustration board　d. Gouache　g. YAESU PUBLISHING CO., LTD.　h. Tomoaki Kotani　＊Since I had to illustrate this forthcoming car before its announcement, I spent the most time to analyze informations. I think I guess it right.. in 95 percent.

a. 自動車　b. オリジナル　c. ハレパネ　d. リキテックス、ロットリング　e. 350㍉×500㍉　f. 1985年　h. 稲垣謙治　　a. CAR　b. Original work　c. Panel　d. Liquitex and rotring pen　h. Kenji Inagaki

a. 1800～2000乗用車予想図　b. 自動車専門誌新車予想企
画　c. イラストボード　d. ガッシュ　e. 350㎜×500㎜
f. 1979年　g. 八重州出版　h. 小谷智昭　＊旧モデル、他
のライバルモデルなどと、時代のトレンドを計算に入れて
制作した。

a. PROVISIONAL LAUREL MARK II　b. Editorial for
magazine　c. Illustration board　d. Gouache　g. YAESU
PUBLISHING CO., LTD.　h. Tomoaki Kotani　＊I
produced it considering the style of the previous or other
rival models and trend at those times.

a. シボレーベルエア　コンバーチブル　b. オリジナル
c. クレセントボード No.310　d. リキテックス　e. 364㎜×
515㎜　f. 1984年　h. 相川修一

a. CHEVROLET BEL AIR CONVERTIBLE　b. Original
work　c. Crescent board #310　d. Liquitex　h. Shuichi
Aikawa

a. イエローキャブ　b. 雑誌表紙　c. クレセントボード
No.310　d. アクリル　e. 520㎜×350㎜　f. 1984年　g. 電
波新聞社　h. 青木正明　＊実際にニューヨークで自分で撮
って来た写真を資料にしました。

a. YELLOW CAB　b. Magazine cover　c. Crescent
board ＃310　d. Acrylic　g. DENPA PUBLICATIONS,
INC.　h. Masaaki Aoki　＊Reference source was a
photograph which I took in New York.

a. ビュイック スカイラーク b. JAAA展 c. クレセン
トボード №115 d. リキテックス e. 515㎜×710㎜ f.
1985年 h. 中村 信 ＊ロサンゼルス市内の風景，自分で
撮った写真を資料にした。

a. BUICK SKYLARK b. Exhibited work c. Crescent
board #115 d. Liquitex h. Shin Nakamura ＊ The
location is inside Los Angeles city. Referenced is the
picture I took.

a. 堂々フォード b. カタログ c. B.B.ケント（細目）
d. リキテックス e. 400㎜×610㎜ f. 1985年 g. オート
ラマ h. 細川武志 ＊1920年代にタイムスリップした
Probe V, 古い写真のイメージという注文があった。

a. FORD BEING FORWARD b. Catalog c. Kent paper
d. Liquitex g. AUTRAMA, INC. h. Takeshi Hosokawa ＊Commissioned image was that "Timeslipped
Probe V into the '20th".

a. コルベット1961　b. オリジナル　c. キャンソン紙　d.
ドローイング・インキ　e. 515㎜×364㎜　f. 1984年　h.
永野清貴　＊自画像……かな？

a. CORVETTE 1961　b. Original work　c. Canson paper
d. Drawing ink　h. Kiyotaka Nagano　＊My portrait／
... hopefully.

a. ポルシェ356　b. プラモデルパッケージ　c. クレセン
トボード №100　d. リキテックス　e. 300㎜×400㎜　f.
1981年　g. トミー工業　h. 細川武志　＊パッケージの仕
事は初めてだったので少しリキみ過ぎて少しきゅうくつな
イラストになってしまった。

a. PORSCHE 356　b. Package for plastic model　c. Crescent board #100　d. Liquitex　g. TOMY KOGYO, INC.
h. Takeshi Hosokawa　＊Because the package illustration was commissioned for the first time, I strained too
much. So this work was rather tight, I was afraid.

a. バラードyou b. レコードジャケット c. コンピュータ・グラフィックス f. 1985年 g. RVC h. 岡本　博

a. BALLADE FOR YOU b. Record jacket c. Computer graphics g. RVC CORPORATION h. Hiroshi Okamoto

a. ホンダスポーツS600　b. パッケージ　c. イラストボード　d. アクリル, ガッシュ　e. 275㎜×400㎜　f. 1985年　g. エルエス　h. 鴨下示佳　＊このシリーズは何枚も描きましたが, 往時を思い出し懐しく, 楽しみながら仕上げました。

a. HONDA SPORT S600　b. Package illustration　c. Illustration board　d. Acrylic and gouache　g. L&S CO., LTD.　h. Tokiyoshi Kamoshita　＊As I particulary like this type of cars, I really enjoyed illustrating it which reminded me of my younger days.

a. ポルシェ911カレラ'85　b. プラモデルパッケージ　c. クレセントボード No215　d. リキテックス　e. 364㎜×515㎜　f. 1985年　g. フジミ模型　h. 梅津成美

a. PORSCHE 911 CARRERA '85　b. Package illustration　c. Crescent board #215　d. Liquitex　g. FUJIMI MOKEI CO., LTD.　h. Shigeyoshi Umezu

a. BMWターボ　b. 雑誌の表紙　c. キャンソン紙　d. ドローイングインキ　e. 257㎜×364㎜　f. 1985年　g. リクルート　h. 永野清貴　＊非売品のドイツ車です。

a. BMW TURBO　b. Magazine cover　c. Canson paper d. Drawing ink　g. RECRUIT CO., LTD.　h. Kiyotaka Nagano　＊This German car is not for sale.

a. トヨタMR-2　b. プラモデルのパッケージ　c. イラストボード　d. アクリル、ガッシュ　e. 360㎜×590㎜　f. 1984年　g. エルエス　h. 鴨下示佳　＊車が発売されて間もなく描きました。話題の車だったので関心を持って仕上げました。

a. TOYOTA MR-2　b. Package illustration for plastic model　c. Illustration board　d. Acrylic and gouache　g. L&S CO., LTD.　h. Tokiyoshi Kamoshita　＊I have illustrated this work soon after the automobile went on market. As this type was the topic of that time, I had completed it with strong interest.

a. 1957年キャデラック　エルドラド　ブロウアム　b.『ク
ラシックCAR』画集（未発表）　c. ケントボード　d. ポス
ターカラー，ガッシュ，アクリル　e. 730㍉×630㍉　f.
1986年　h. 野口佐武郎　＊豪華なクラシックカーとなると
資料が少なく，限定される様になり，資料集めに苦労しま
す。

a. 1957 CADILLAC ELDORADO BROUGHAM b.
Unpublished c. Kent board d. Poster color, gouache,
and acrylic h. Saburo Noguchi ＊The more grand classic cars we decided to draw, the more restricted the
references were.

a. トヨタ　MR2　b. 海外向け広告　c. パネル貼りケン
ト紙　d. 水彩　e. 600㎜×700㎜　f. 1984年　g. U.S.トヨ
タ　h. 猪本義弘

a. TOYOTA MR2　b. Advertisement for US market　c
. Paper and panel d. Watercolor g. U.S. TOYOTA
MOTOR, INC.　h. Yoshihiro Inomoto

カースタイリング
&
パワー・パーツ

CAR STYLING & POWER PARTS

TOYOTA MR2

TOYOTA

a．トヨタABフェートン　b．海外用カレンダー　c．パネ
ル貼りケント紙　d．水彩　e．610㎜×810㎜　f．1983年
g．トヨタ自動車　h．猪本義弘

a. TOYOTA AB PHOETON　b. Calendar for overseas
c. Paper and panel　d. Watercolor　g. TOYOTA
MOTOR CORPORATION　h. Yoshihiro Inomoto

a．トヨタ　スープラ　b．海外用カレンダー　c．パネル貼
りケント紙　d．水彩　e．680㎜×820㎜　f．1983年　g．ト
ヨタ自動車　h．猪本義弘

a. TOYOTA SUPRA　b. Calendar for overseas　c.
Paper and panel　d. Watercolor　g. TOYOTA MOTOR
CORPORATION　h. Yoshihiro Inomoto

a. 日産キューエックス　b. 第26回東京モーターショー用
カタログ　c. B.B.ケント（細目）　d. ホルベイン水彩, リキ
テックス　e. 450㎜×750㎜　f. 1985年　g. 日産自動車
h. 小野直宣

a. NISSAN CUE-X　b. Catalogue for the motor show
c. B.B. Kent paper　d. Watercolor and liquitex　g. NIS-
SAN MOTOR CO., LTD.　h. Naonobu Ono

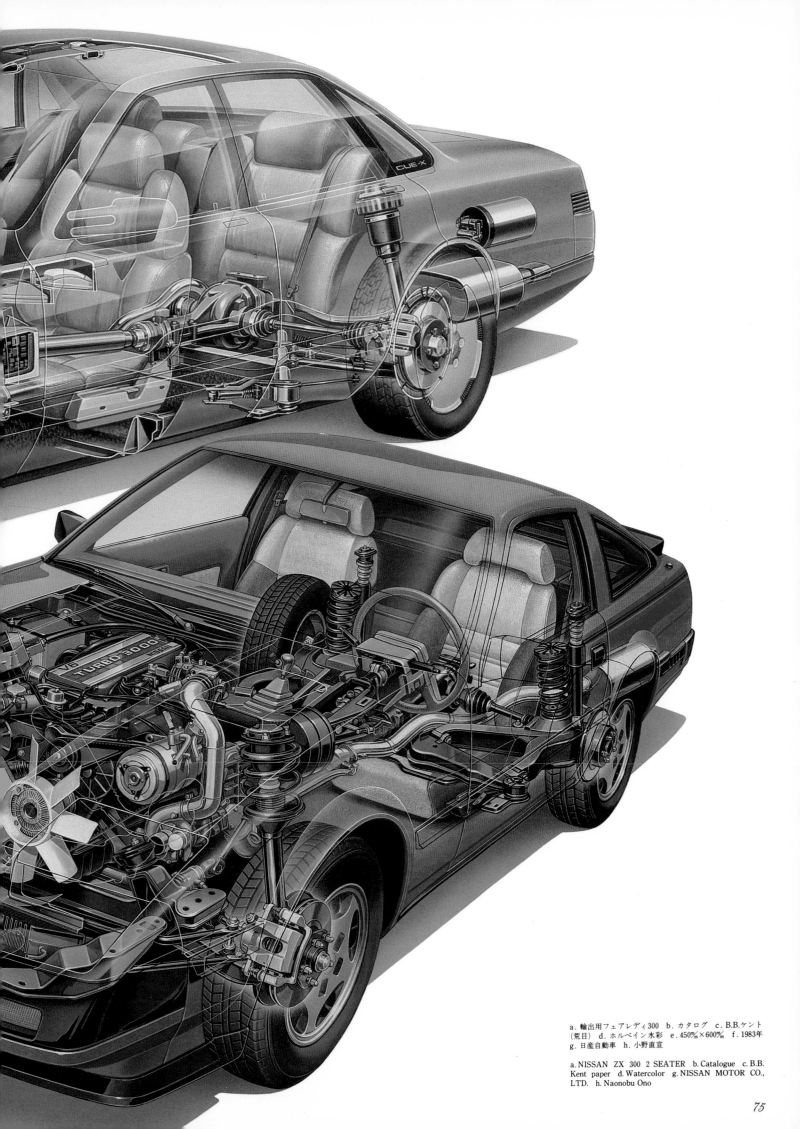

a. 輸出用フェアレディ300　b. カタログ　c. B.B.ケント
（荒目）　d. ホルベイン水彩　e. 450㎜×600㎜　f. 1983年
g. 日産自動車　h. 小野直宣

a. NISSAN ZX 300 2 SEATER　b. Catalogue　c. B.B.
Kent paper　d. Watercolor　g. NISSAN MOTOR CO.,
LTD.　h. Naonobu Ono

a. トヨタ ソアラ b. カタログ＆ポスター c. パネル貼
リケント紙 d. 水彩 e. 700㎜×890㎜ f. 1985年 g. ト
ヨタ自動車 h. 猪本義弘

a. TOYOTA SOARER b. Catalog and poster c. Paper
and panel d. Watercolor g. TOYOTA MOTOR COR-
PORATION h. Yoshihiro Inomoto

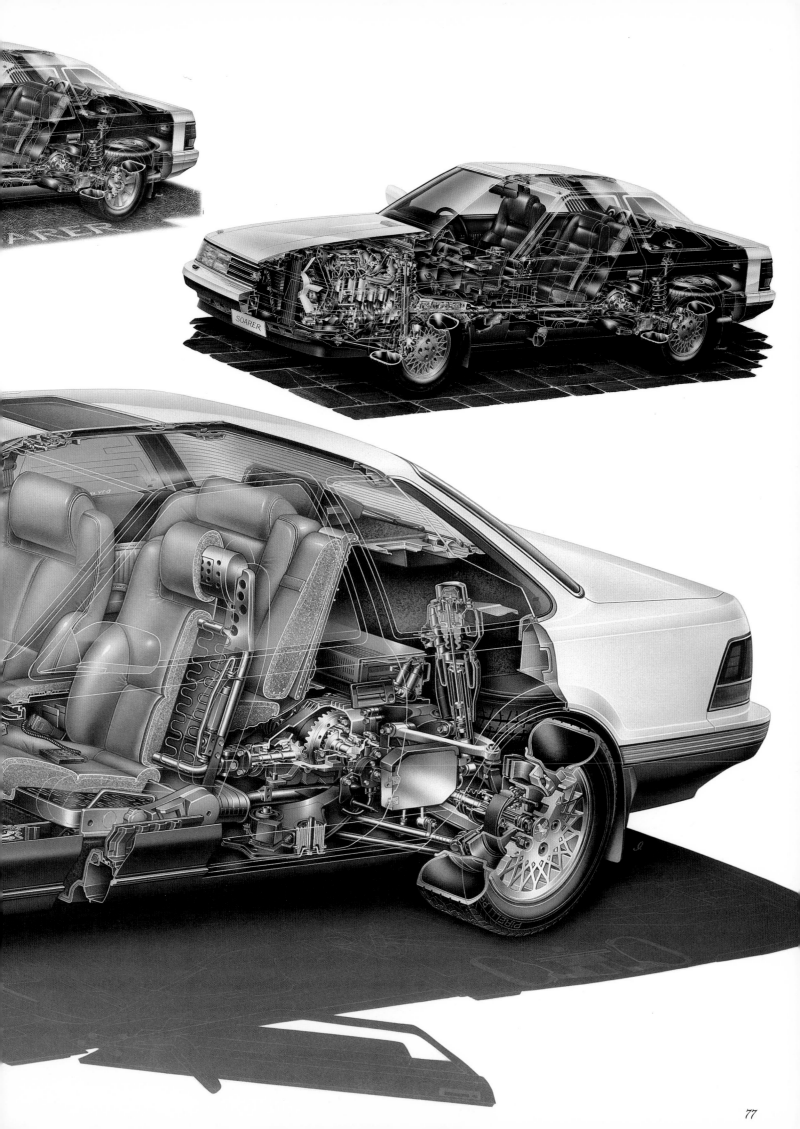

a. 1931ブガッティタイプ53　b. 雑誌『ロード＆トラック』
c. パネル貼りケント紙　d. 水彩　e. 620㎜×820㎜　f.
1983年　g. CBS (U.S.A.)　h. 猪本義弘

a. 1931 BUGATTI TYPE 53　b. Editorial for "Road and
Truck" magazine　c. Paper and panel　d. Watercolor
g. CBS PUBLICATIONS　h. Yoshihiro Inomoto

a.1926 ブガッティタイプ37GP　b.『構造画への招待』作
品集　c.ケント紙　d.ペン&インキ　e.650㍉×700㍉
f.1974年　g.二玄社　h.猪本義弘

a.1926 BUGATTI TYPE 37GP　b.Portfolio　c.Kent
paper　d.Pen & ink　g.NIGENSHA PUBLISHING　h.
Yoshihiro Inomoto

a. 輸出用ローレル　b. カタログ　c. B.B.ケント（荒目）
d. ホルベイン水彩　e. 450㎜×700㎜　f. 1984年　g. 日産
自動車　h. 小野直宣

a. NISSAN LAUREL　b. Catalogue　c. B.B. Kent paper
d. Watercolor　g. NISSAN MOTOR CO., LTD.　h.
Naonobu Ono

a. ホンダ　バラード　b. カタログ　c. B.B.ケントボード
d. ガッシュ　e. 515㎜×728㎜　f. 1985年　g. 本田技研工
業　h. 斉藤　信　＊一部写真との合成。

a. HONDA BALLADE　b. Catalog　c. Kent board　d.
Gouache　g. HONDA MOTOR CORPORATION　h.
Shin Saito　＊A part of details is a collage with photo-
graph.

a. デューセンバーグSSJ　b. カレンダー　c. 厚ロトレーシングペーパー　d. ロットリング，丸ペン　e. 475㎜×760㎜　f. 1981年　g. ブリヂストン　h. 矢野富士嶺
＊とにかく時間がかかる。1度使用された後暇をみて，手を加えました。

a. DUESENBERG SSJ　b. Calendar　c. Tracing paper d. Rotring pen and pen　g. BRIDGESTONE CORPORA-TION　h. Fujine Yano　＊It took me much time. After publishing, I retouched it while I found the time to do.

a. 1914 マーサー　レースアバウト　b. 『構造画への招
待』作品集　c. ケント紙　d. ペン＆インキ　e. 650㍉×
700㍉　f. 1973年　g. 二玄社　h. 猪本義弘

a. 1914 MERCER RACEABOUT　b. Portfolio　c. Kent
paper　d. Pen & ink　g. NIGENSHA PUBLISHING　h.
Yoshihiro Inomoto

a. マツダRX-7　b. カタログ&ポスター　c. パネル貼り
ケント紙　d. 水彩　e. 650㎜×850㎜　f. 1985年　g. マツ
ダ自動車　h. 猪本義弘

a. MAZDA RX-7　b. Catalog and poster　c. paper and
panel　d. Watercolor　g. MAZDA MOTOR CORPORA-
TION　h. Yoshihiro Inomoto

a. サバンナRX-7（国内仕様）　b. カタログ&ポスター
c. パネル貼りケント紙　d. 水彩　e. 650㎜×850㎜　f.
1985年　g. マツダ自動車　h. 猪本義弘

a. SAVANNA RX-7　b. Catalog and poster　c. Paper
and panel　d. Watercolor　g. MAZDA MOTOR COR-
PORATION　h. Yoshihiro Inomoto

a. ロータスエランS3　b. カレンダー　c. B.B.ケントボード　d. デザイナーズカラー　e. 515㍉×720㍉　f. 1983年　g. ブリヂストン　h. 矢野富士嶺

a. LOTUS ELAN S3 b. Calendar c. Kent board d. Designers color g. BRIDGESTONE CORPORATION h. Fujine Yano

a. ランサーEX　b. カタログ　c. パントン紙　d. ニュートンガッシュ他　e. 420㍉×700㍉　f. 1980年　g. 三菱自動車工業　h. 初谷秀雄　＊主に手法として，エアブラシと面相筆を用いて描いた。

a. LANCER EX b. Catalog c. Pantone color paper d. Gouache g. MITSUBISHI MOTORS CO., LTD. h. Hideo Hatsugai ＊Used medium were sable brushes and airbrush

a. トヨエース　トラック　b. カタログ　c. クレセントボ
ード No.210　d. リキテックス　e. 600㎜×1000㎜　f. 1985
年　g. トヨタ自動車　h. 石崎康秀

a. TOYOACE TRUCK　b. Catalogue　c. Crescent board
#210　d. Liquitex　g. TOYOTA MOTOR CORPORA-
TION　h. Yasuhide Ishizaki

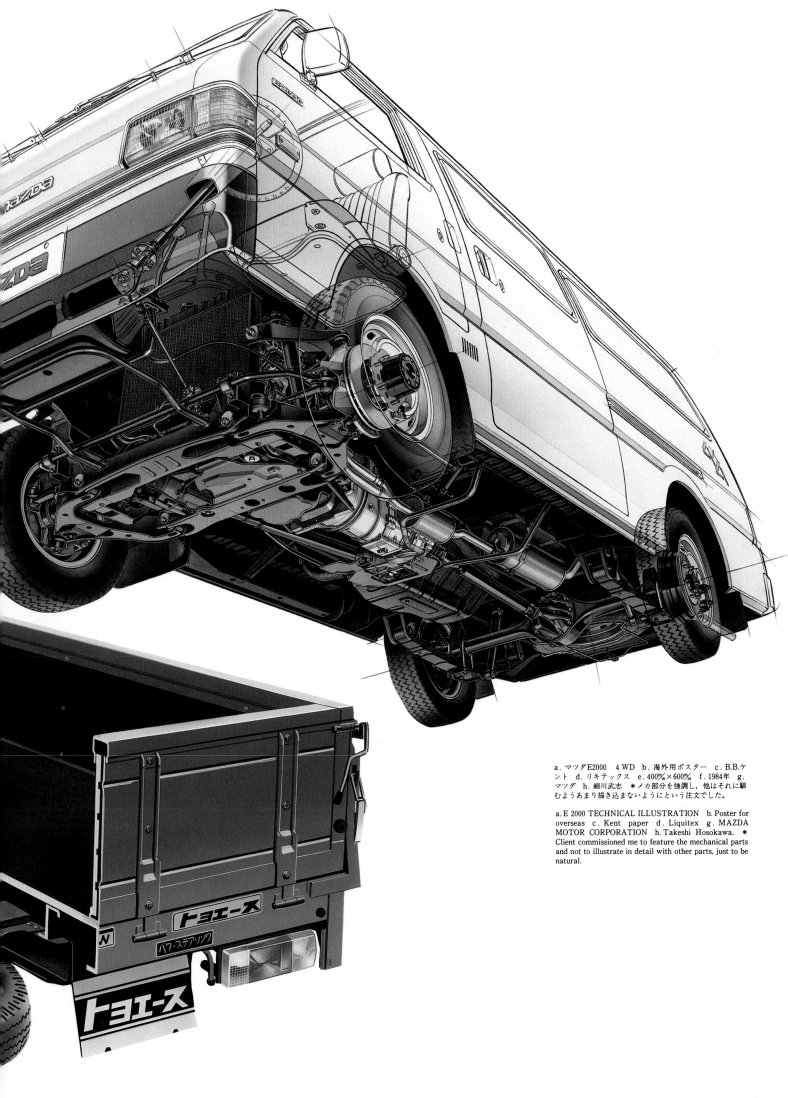

a. マツダE2000　4WD　b. 海外用ポスター　c. B.B.ケント　d. リキテックス　e. 400㍉×600㍉　f. 1984年　g. マツダ　h. 細川武志　＊メカ部分を強調し、他はそれに馴むようあまり描き込まないようにという注文でした。

a. E 2000 TECHNICAL ILLUSTRATION　b. Poster for overseas　c. Kent　paper　d. Liquitex　g. MAZDA MOTOR CORPORATION　h. Takeshi Hosokawa.　＊ Client commissioned me to feature the mechanical parts and not to illustrate in detail with other parts, just to be natural.

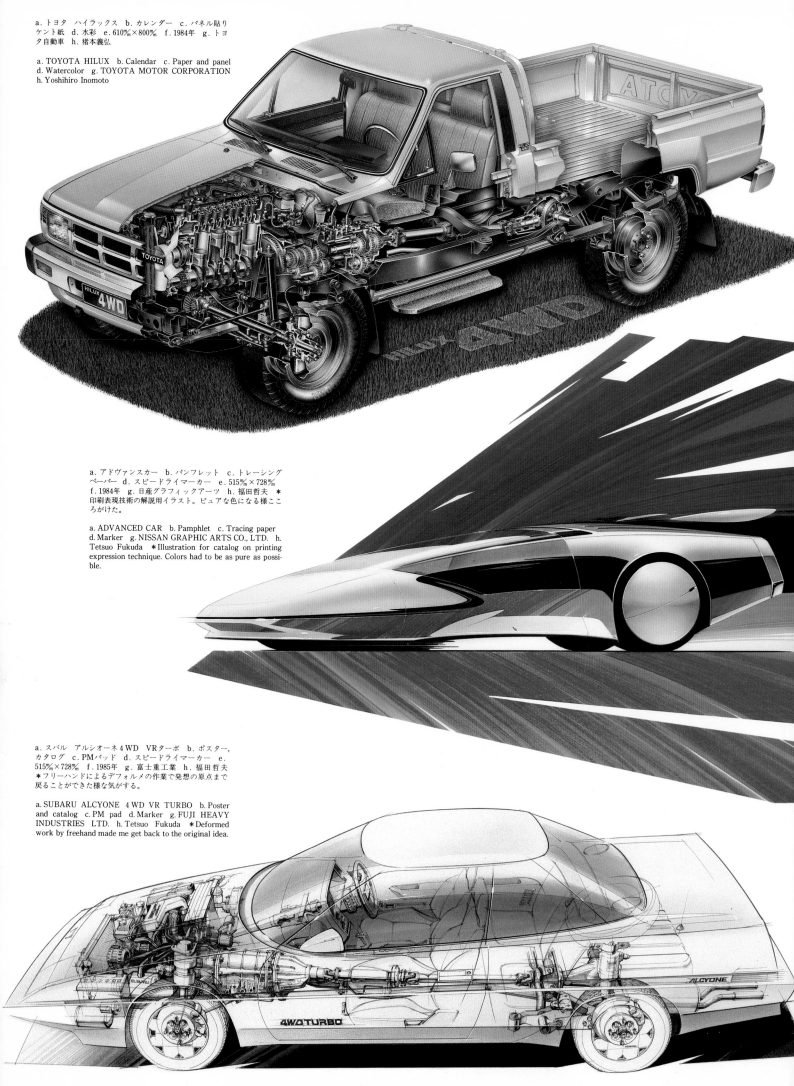

a. トヨタ ハイラックス b. カレンダー c. パネル貼り
ケント紙 d. 水彩 e. 610㎜×800㎜ f. 1984年 g. トヨ
タ自動車 h. 猪本義弘

a. TOYOTA HILUX b. Calendar c. Paper and panel
d. Watercolor g. TOYOTA MOTOR CORPORATION
h. Yoshihiro Inomoto

a. アドヴァンスカー b. パンフレット c. トレーシング
ペーパー d. スピードライマーカー e. 515㎜×728㎜
f. 1984年 g. 日産グラフィックアーツ h. 福田哲夫 ＊
印刷表現技術の解説用イラスト。ピュアな色になる様ここ
ろがけた。

a. ADVANCED CAR b. Pamphlet c. Tracing paper
d. Marker g. NISSAN GRAPHIC ARTS CO., LTD. h.
Tetsuo Fukuda ＊Illustration for catalog on printing
expression technique. Colors had to be as pure as possible.

a. スバル アルシオーネ4WD VRターボ b. ポスター,
カタログ c. PMパッド d. スピードライマーカー e.
515㎜×728㎜ f. 1985年 g. 富士重工業 h. 福田哲夫
＊フリーハンドによるデフォルメの作業で発想の原点まで
戻ることができた様な気がする。

a. SUBARU ALCYONE 4WD VR TURBO b. Poster
and catalog c. PM pad d. Marker g. FUJI HEAVY
INDUSTRIES LTD. h. Tetsuo Fukuda ＊Deformed
work by freehand made me get back to the original idea.

a. フェザント3000M　b. オリジナル　c. NT紙　d. パステル他　e. 590㍉×840㍉　f. 1986年　h. 初谷秀雄　＊オリジナルデザインの2シーターで全高970㍉の車。背景に気を配った。

a. PHEASANT 3000M　b. Original work　c. NT paper
d. Pastel　h. Hideo Hatsugai　＊Two-seaters and 970㍉
at body height. Background is carefully arranged.

a. アドバンスカー　b. オリジナル　c. PMパッド　d. スピードライマーカー　e. 364㍉×515㍉　f. 1986年　h. 福田哲夫　＊某電装品会社の製品イメージ・コンセプトスケッチの為のスタイリング・エクササイズ。

a. ADVANCED CAR　b. Original work　c. PM pad　d.
Marker　h. Tetsuo Fukuda　＊Image conept sketch of
the electric parts for the related company. This work was
drawn as styling exercise.

a. アドバンスカー　b. オリジナル　c. PM パッド　d. スピードライマーカー　e. 364㍉×515㍉　f. 1986年　h. 福田哲夫　＊某電装品の会社の製品イメージ・コンセプトスケッチの為のスタイリング・エクササイズ。

a. ADVANCED CAR　b. Original work　c. PM pad　d.
Marker　h. Tetsuo Fukuda　＊Image concept sketch of
the electric parts for the related company. This work was
drawn as styling exercise.

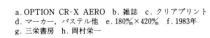

a. OPTION CR-X AERO　b. 雑誌　c. クリアプリント
d. マーカー, パステル他　e. 180㍉×420㍉　f. 1983年
g. 三栄書房　h. 岡村栄一

a. OPTION CR-X AERO　b. Magazine　c. Clear print
d. Marker and pastel　g. SANEI SHOBO CO., LTD.　h.
Eiichi Okamura

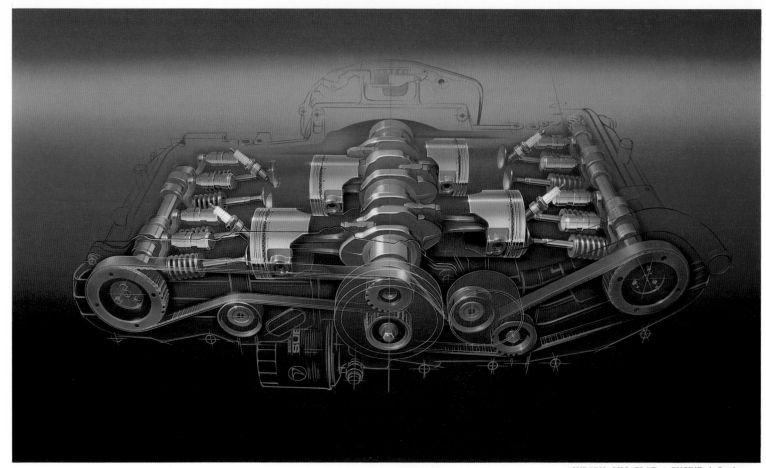

a. スバル水平対向 4 気筒エンジン　b. カタログ　c. クレセントボード No.205　d. リキテックス　e. 515㍉×728㍉　f. 1985年　g. 富士重工業　h. 福田哲夫　*駆動部分のみの省略した表現方法で，テクニカルイメージを伝える。

a. SUBARU OHC FLAT-4 ENGINE　b. Catalog　c. Crescent board #205　d. Liqutex　g. FUJI HEAVY IN-DUSTRIES LTD.　h. Tetsuo Fukuda　* Technical image was informed with the expression of the wheel-driven parts. Other details were skipped.

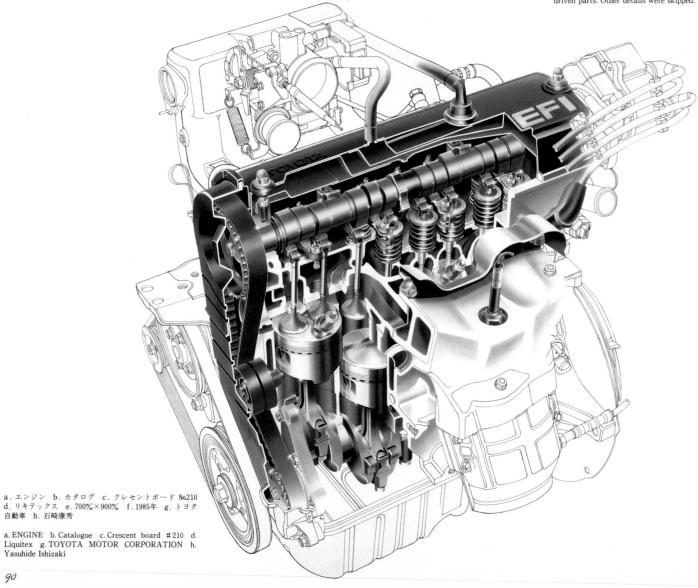

a. エンジン　b. カタログ　c. クレセントボード No.210　d. リキテックス　e. 700㍉×900㍉　f. 1985年　g. トヨタ自動車　h. 石崎康秀

a. ENGINE　b. Catalogue　c. Crescent board #210　d. Liquitex　g. TOYOTA MOTOR CORPORATION　h. Yasuhide Ishizaki

a. PLASMA-VE・X V 6 ツインカム・24V・ツインターボ
b. 第26回東京モーターショー用カタログ　c. B.B.ケント
（細目）　d. ホルベイン水彩，リキテックス　e. 450㎜×
600㎜　f. 1985年　g. 日産自動車　h. 小野直宣

a. VG30 PROTO　b. Catalogue for the motor show　c.
B.B. kent paper　d. Watercolor and liquitex　g. NIS-
SAN MOTOR CO., LTD.　h. Naonobu Ono

a. エンジン（スリーバルブ）　b. カタログ　c. クレセント
ボード №205　d. リキテックス，他　e. 300㎜×360㎜
f. 1959年　g. トヨタ自動車　h. 吉田和弘

a. ENGINE, 3-VALVE　b. Catalog　c. Crescent board
#205　d. Liquitex and mixed media　g. TOYOTA
MOTOR CORPORATION　h. Kazuhiro Yoshida

a.無題　b.オリジナル　c.クレセントボード No.100　d.
リキテックス　e.180㎜×220㎜　f.1982年　h.大内　誠
＊自らドライヴァーとなった時，車を客観的に見れる物は
メーターしなかい。

a. Untitled　b. Original work　c. Crescent board ＃100
d. Liquitex　h. Makoto Ouchi　＊We see a car as an
object only by meters when driving.

a.MRⅡ（エンジン　T−VIS）　b.カタログ　c.B.B.ケ
ント　d.リキテックス，ガッシュ　e.250㎜×350㎜　f.
1984年　g.トヨタ自動車　h.中島　秀　＊描くことより，
どう表現するかに頭を悩ました。

a. MR-Ⅱ enging T-VIS　b. Catalog　c. Kent paper　d.
Liquitex and gouache　g. TOYOTA MOTOR CORPOR-
ATION　h. Hide Nakajima　＊What I most cared about
was not how to draw, but how to express.

a. フェラーリ250 GTO b. オリジナル c. クレセント
ボード No.100 d. リキテックス, デザイナーズカラー e.
400㎜×310㎜ f.1985年 h. 大内 誠 *フェラーリの
本『ベルリネッタフェラーリ』より2カットを参考にする。

a. FERRARI 250 GTO b. Original work c. Crescent
board #100 d. Liquitex and designers color h. Makoto
Ouchi *I used two illustrations inside a Ferrari book,
"Berlinetta Ferrari 1" as the base.

a. 夕暮れpartⅡ　b. オリジナル　c. クレセントボード
d. アクリル絵具, ガッシュ　e. 450㍉×320㍉　f. 1985年
h. 坂口 学　＊300SLとの連作で現代のスポーツカーを描
いてみました。

a. AT TWILIGHT ＃2　b. Original work　c. Illustration board　d. Acrylic and gouache　h. Manabu Sakaguchi　＊As the 2nd work continued from the 300SL I have drawn a modern sports car.

a. メルセデス・ベンツ　b. 雑誌表紙　c. クレセントボード No.310　d. アクリル　e. 570㍉×380㍉　f. 1984年　g. 電波新聞社　h. 青木正明　＊某駐車場にあったベンツが資料になってしまいました。

a. MERCEDES BENZ　b. Magazine cover　c. Créscent board ＃310　d. Acrylic　g. DEMPA PUBLICATIONS, INC.　h. Masaaki Aoki　＊Reference source is a Benz at a parking place.

a. アバルト　シムカ1300　b. オリジナル　c. オリオンプ
ロフェッショナルボード　d. リキテックス　e. 293㍉×
200㍉　f. 1985年　h. 榎本竹利

a. ABARTH SIMCA 1300　b. Original work　c. Orion Professional board　d. Liquitex　h. Taketoshi Enomoto.

a. 夕暮れ　b. オリジナル　c. クレセントボード　d. アクリル絵具, ガッシュ　e. 340㍉×280㍉　f. 1985年　h. 坂口 学　＊メルセデス・ベンツ300SL. 作画にあたっての資料に花岡弘明氏の御協力を頂きました。

a. AT TWILIGHT　b. Original work　c. Illustration board　d. Acrylic and gouache　h. Manabu Sakaguchi　＊The model is Mercedes Benz 300SL. Mr. Hiroaki Hanaoka kindly collaborated with me on it.

a . ビー　エム　ダブリュー　b . 雑誌表紙　c . クレセント
ボード No.310　d . アクリル　e . 560㎜×380㎜　f . 1984年
g . 電波新聞社　h . 青木正明　＊資料写真は中古車屋さん
の店頭でドキドキしながら撮りました。

a . BMW　b . Magazine cover　c . Crescent board ＃310
d . Acrylic　g . DEMPA PUBLɅTIONS, INC.　h .
Masaaki Aoki　＊I took its reference photo in a used-
car shop.

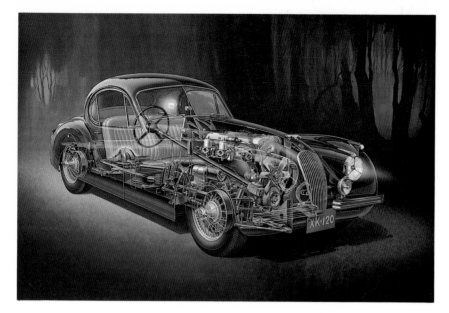

a. 1953年型ジャガーXK120フィックスド ヘッド クーペ
b. オリジナル　c. B.B.ケント（荒目）　d. ホルベイン水彩
e. 450㎜×600㎜ (right), 600㎜×900㎜ (upper)　f. 1984年
h. 小野直宣　＊XK120が好きでイギリスから取り寄せた
時，記念に描いた。

a. 1953 JAGUAR　XK120 FIXED‐HEAD‐COUPE b.
Original　work　c. B.B.Kent　paper　d. Watercolor　h.
Naonobu Ono　＊XK120 has been my favourite car for a
long time. So one day I decided to buy it and actually did.
This work was a memorial for my purchase.

クラシック・カー

CLASSIC CARS

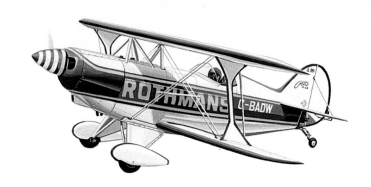

a. モーガン プラス8 b. プラモデルパッケージ c. ミューズKMKケント d. ニッカポスターカラー他 e. 500㎜×800㎜ f. 1982年 g. エルエス h. 佐竹政夫 ＊実用的でない車ほど魅力が有るのはなぜでしょう。

a. MORGAN PLUS 8'S b. Plastic model package c. Kent paper d. Poster color g. L&S CO., LTD. h. Masao Satake ＊It's strange, sometimes the more unpractical the car is, the more attractive it is.

a. 1932年型ロールス・ロイス ファンタムII b. オリジナル c. クレセントボード №310 d. リキテックス e. 364㎜×515㎜ f. 1985年 h. 三五英夫 ＊1930年代の英国独特の重厚な伝統を表現してみた。全体の色に苦労しました。

a. 1932 ROLLS - ROYCE PHANTOM II b. Original work c. Crescent board ＃310 d. Liquitex h. Hideo Sango ＊I intended to express a dignified tradition of U. K. in the 30's. I also made a serious efforts on the whole color balances.

a. ランチェスター b. オリジナル c. アイボリー紙 №940 d. ホルベインカラーインク e. 305㎜×214㎜ f. 1985年 h. 三五英夫

a. LANCHESTER b. Original work c. Ivory paper ＃940 d. Color ink h. Hideo Sango

a.1934 E.R.Aイングランド　b.『クラシック・カー』画
集（未発表）　c.ケントボード　d.ポスターカラー，アク
リル　e.350㎜×600㎜　f.1984年　h.野口佐武郎　＊英
国車にふさわしい英国の建物を！　よい背景の資料がある
と仕事は楽しみです。

a.1934　E.R.A.　ENGLAND　b. Unpublished　c. Kent
board　d. Poster color and Acrylic　h. Saburo Noguchi
＊The gorgeous English car has to be illustrated against
the gorgeous surroundings！ I feel happy to work with a
reference of good backgrounds.

a. ジャガーSS100　b. オリジナル　c. クレセントボード
No.114　d. サクラマット水彩，カラーインク　e. 510㎜×
720㎜　h. 斎藤　寿

a. JAGUAR SS100　b. Original work　c. Crescent board
#114　d. Watercolor and color ink　h. Hisashi Saito

a. フレイザーナッシュ：ルマン・レプリカ　b. オリジナル
c. キャンソン紙　d. パステル他　e. 520㎜×700㎜　f.
1985年　h. 井川友晴

a. FRAZER NASH：LE MANS REPLICA　b. Original
work　c. Canson　paper　d. Pastel, etc.　h. Tomoharu
Ikawa

a. VIP Car　b. 雑誌　c. B.B.ケント　d. リキテックス　e. 150㍉×250㍉　f. 1981年　g. マガジンハウス　h. 細川武志　＊淡彩で柔らかく仕上げてみた。

a. VIP CAR　b. Magazine illustration　c. Kent paper　d. Liquitex　g. MAGAZINE HOUSE LTD.　h. Takeshi Hosokawa　＊I finished it with soft pastel tone.

a. アルファロメオ b. オリジナル c. クレセントボード
No.114 d. サクラマット水彩 e. 510㎜×720㎜ h. 斎藤
寿

a. ALFA ROMEO b. Original work c. Crescent board
#114 d. Watercolor h. Hisashi Saito

a. ヒストリー オブ ポンティアック b. カー・マガジン
c. クレセントボード No.300 d. カラーインク e. 364㎜×
515㎜ f. 1985年 g. 二玄社 h. 海勢頭清治

a. HISTORY OF PONTIAC b. Magazine illustration
c. Crescent board ＃300 d. Color ink g. NIGENSHA
PUBLISHING h. Seiji Kaisedo

a. 1932年型オーバン V12 b. オリジナル c. クレセント
ボード №310 d. リキテックス e. 364㎜×515㎜ f.
1985年 h. 三五英夫 ＊霧の中での車と飛行艇をイメージ
に淡い色相で光と影を出せたらと苦労した。

a. 1932 AUBURN V12 b. Original work c. Crescent
board ＃310 d. Liquitex h. Hideo Sango ＊With an
image of an automobile and flying boat I concentrated on
the expression of light and shade in a pale tone.

a. アルファロメオ 8 C 2600 b. オリジナル c. クレセン
トボード №100 d. リキテックス e. 364㎜×515㎜ f.
1984年 h. 森 優 ＊個展用に描いた作品。エアブラシを
使用。ザ・レグレティスト・カーを参考。

a. ALFA ROMEO 8 C 2600 b. Original work c. Cresent
board ＃100 d. Liquitex h. Yu Mori ＊This work was
for my one-man, show completed with airbrush. Reference source was a book called "The Greatest Cars".

a. 1915　ハドソン　b. クラシックカー画集用　c. ケント
ボード　d. ポスターカラー，アクリル　e. 350㎜×600㎜
f. 1982年　h. 野口佐武郎　＊産業革命発生地，英国の車だ
な〜，と感じるものが出したかったのですが……。

a. 1915 HUDSON　b. Unpublished　c. Kent board　d.
poster color and acrylic　h. Saburo Noguchi　＊I wish to
express an aesthetic atmosphere of England, the birth-
place of the Industrial Revolution.

a. MG　K3　b. オリジナル　c. クレセントボード　No.114
d. リキテックス，サクラマット水彩　e. 510㎜×720㎜
h. 斎藤　寿

a. M.G. K3　b. Original work　c. Crescent board #114
d. Liquitex and watercolor　h. Hisashi Saito

a. ヒルマン1913年型　b. オリジナル　c. ワトソンボード
e. 460㍉×530㍉　f. 1985年　h. 上田毅八郎　＊メカニカ
ルな美しさに魅了されヴィンテージカーの書籍を参考に描
きました。

a. HILLMAN 1913　b. Original work　c. Watson board
h. Kihachiro Ueda　＊I was struck by the mechanical
beauty of the vintage cars.

a. エム・ジー・ティー・エイ　b. オリジナル　c. ヴィンセ
ントヴェラム　d. マジック・マーカー、プリスマパステル
他　e. 530㍉×680㍉　f. 1978年　h. 児玉英雄　＊MG・
TAを所有する友達へのプレゼントに描いたものです。

a. MG・TA　b. Original work　c. Vellum paper　d. Marker and pastel　h. Hideo Kodama　＊This work was
illustrated to give my friend who has owned the MG・
TA.

a. メルセデスベンツSSK　b. オリジナル　c. クレセント
ボード No.114　d. リキテックス　e. 510㎜×720㎜　h. 斎
藤 寿

a. MERCEDES-BENZ SSK　b. Original work　c. Crescent board ＃114　d. Liquitex　h. Hisashi Saito

a. ロータススーパー7　b. 展覧会用　c. クレセントボード No.300　d. カラーインク　e. 364㎜×515㎜　f. 1985年　h. 海勢頭清治

a. LOTUS SUPER 7　b. Exhibition　c. Crescent board ＃300　d. Color ink　h. Seiji Kaisedo

a. メルセデスベンツ300SCロードスター b. オリジナル
c. クレセントボード No.205 d. リキテックス他 e.
260㎜×370㎜ f. 1986年 h. 吉田和弘 ＊Mercedes for
the roadを参考にした。

a. MERCEDES BENZ 300SC ROADSTER b. Original
work c. Crescent board ＃205 d. Liquitex and mixed
media h. Kazuhiro Yoshida ＊I took a reference from
"Mercedes for the Road"

a. 無題 b. オリジナル c. クレセントボード No.100 d.
ペリカンドローイングインキ e. 364㎜×515㎜ f. 1986
年 h. 末広治信

a. UNTITLED b. Original work c. Crescent board
＃100 d. Drawing ink h. Harunobu Suehiro

a．カワサキGPZ750ターボ　b．ポスター　c．クレセント
ボード No.100　d．デザイナーズカラー　e．500㍉×750㍉
f．1983年　g．川崎重工業　h．寿福隆志　＊ターボのメカ
ニズムを見せる事とマシンの迫力を出す為にローアングル
にしてみた。

a. KAWASAKI GPZ 750 TURBO　b. Poster　c. Crescent
board ＃100　d. Disigners　color　g. KAWASAKI
HEAVY INDUSTRIES, LTD.　h. Takashi Jufuku
＊Main purpose is to show a mechanism of the turbo and
a powerful machine of strong appealing. So I did this
work from the low angle.

バイク

MOTORBIKES

a. スズキ GSX-R750 b. カタログ c. クレセントボード
№110 d. リキテックス, ガッシュ e. 510㎜×620㎜ f.
1984年 g. 鈴木自動車工業 h. 中島 秀 ＊全体写真が
ないので光のバランスに苦労した。

a. SUZUKI GSX-R750 b. Catalog c. Crescent board
#110 d. Liquitex and gouache g. SUZUKI MOTOR
CO., LTD. h. Hide Nakajima ＊As a photograph of
whole body was not supplied, I made really serious
efforts on the balance of light.

a. スズキGSX-R750 b. カタログ c. 厚ロトレーシング
ペーパー d. ロットリングペン e. 415㎜×310㎜ f.
1984年 g. 鈴木自動車工業 h. 鳴岡五郎

a. SUZUKI GSX-R750 b. Catalog c. Tracing paper
d. Rotring pen g. SUZUKI MOTOR CO., LTD. h. Goro
Shimaoka

a. スズキGSX-R 750 (エンジン) b. カタログ c. 厚ロ
トレーシングペーパー d. ロットリングペン e. 415㎜×
335㎜ f. 1984年 g. 鈴木自動車工業 h. 鳴岡五郎

a. SUZUKI GSX-R750 (engine) b. Catalog c. Tracing
paper d. Rotring pen g. SUZUKI MOTOR CO., LTD.
h. Goro Shimaoka

a. ヤマハRZ 500　b. カタログ&ポスター　c. クレセント
ボード No.100　d. ニッカーデザイナーズカラー　e.
900㎜×600㎜　f. 1984年　g. ヤマハ発動機　h. 大内　誠
＊どうしても描けないメカを，下に写して描いた。

a. YAMAHA RZ 500　b. Catalogue and poster　c. Crescent board ＃100　d. Designers color　g. YAMAHA
MOTOR LTD.　h. Makoto Ouchi　＊There was single
part I have tried very hard, but never satisfied. Finally I
traced to complete it, as a compromise.

a. ハーレー・ダビッドソンFLX80ローライダー　b. 雑誌
c. ケント紙　d. 水彩絵具　e. 420㎜×590㎜　f. 1978年
g. 文林堂　h. 加地茂裕　＊現車から寸法を測りタンク，シート，等々少々アレンジし描きました。

a. HARLEY - DAVIDSON　LOW　RIDER　b. Magazine
c. Kent paper　d. Watercolor　g. BUNRINDO CO., LTD.
h. Shigehiro Kaji　＊The size of each part was measured
precisely, however the tank and seats were calicatured a
little bit.

a. ヤマハV・max　b. カタログ及びポスター　c. クレセ
ントボード №100　d. ニッカーデザイナーズカラー　e.
600㎜×700㎜　f. 1985年　g. ヤマハ発動機　h. 大内　誠
＊ヤマハの輸出専用の大型バイク。コラーニではないか，と
思わせるデザインは好きだ。

a. YAMAHA V-MAX　b. Catalogue and poster　c. Crescent board ＃100　d. Designers color　g. YAMAHA
MOTOR LTD.　h. Makoto Ouchi　＊Yamaha large-
sized bike for export only. I like this design, slightly
reminded me of Luigi Colani.

a. ホンダCMX250C　b. ショップマニュアル表紙　c. 製版用フィルム　d. アニメックス他　e. 205㎜×285㎜　f. 1985年　g. 本田技研工業　h. 鬼武龍一　＊フィルムにポジ転写して裏からアニメカラーで色入れしたもの。時間短縮には便利。

a. HONDA CMX250C　b. Cover for shop manual　c. Film　d. Animex　g. HONDA MOTOR CO., LTD.　h. Ryuichi Onitake　＊This work was duplicated into positive films and colored by animex from the reverse side of the films. It is convenient way for saving time.

a. ハーレー・ダビッドソン　b. オリジナル　c. スクラッチボード　d. リキテックス他　e. 300㎜×480㎜　f. 1985年　h. 吉田和弘　＊雑誌『サイクルワールド』を参考にした。

a. HARLEY-DAVIDSON　b. Original work　c. Scratch board　d. Liquitex and mixed media　h. Kazuhiro Yoshida　＊From Cycle World magazine.

a. ホンダCBX750F　b. JAAA展　c. トレーシングペーパー　d. ロットリング　e. 220㍉×310㍉　f. 1984年　h. 鬼武龍一　*JAAA展用に、かなり時間をかけて書き上げたもの。0.1㍉3本ダメにしました。

a. HONDA CBX 750 F　b. For exhibition　c. Tracing paper　d. Rotring pen　h. Ryuichi Onitake　*This work took me hard and long time to illustrate. Three pcs. of 0.1 m/m rotring pens were damaged.

a. カワサキ1000R「ニンジャ」　b. プレス・インフォメーション　c. W・トレス　d. ロットリング&スクリーントーン　e. 450㍉×600㍉　f. 1985年　g. 川崎重工業　h. 寿福隆志

a. KAWASAKI 1000 R "NINJA"　b. Press information　c. Double tracing paper　d. Rotring pen and screen tone　g. KAWASAKI HEAVY INDUSTRIES, LTD.　h. Takashi Jufuku

a. 無題　b. オリジナル　c. W・トレーシングペーパー
d. ロットリング（黒）　e. 660㎜×850㎜　f. 1982年　h. 末
広治信

a. UNTITLED　b. Original　work　c. Double　tracing
paper　d. Rotring pen（black）　h. Harunobu Suehiro

a. MVアグスタ750 S　b. オリジナル　c. キャンバスP 20
d. 油彩　e. 530㎜×727㎜　f. 1986年　h. 牧田哲明　＊ど
こまで、MVアグスタの雰囲気が描けたか。いつになったら
この魅力が描けるのか。

a. MV AGUSTA 750 S　b. Original work　c. Canvas　d.
Oil　h. Tetsuaki Makita　＊Did I catch the atmosphere
of thes MV Agusta…Until when did I have to wait for my
ability to reach the peak of portraying its allure…

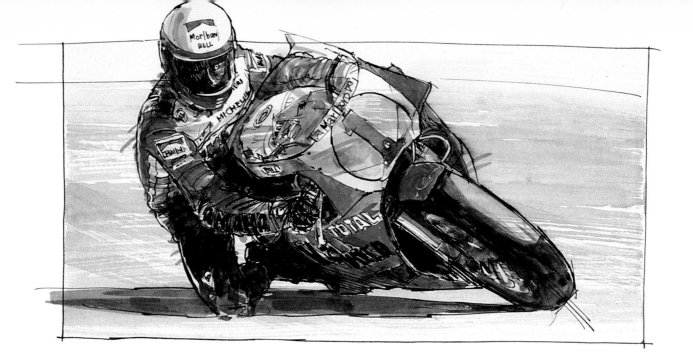

a．ロスマンズ対マルボロ　b．雑誌ピンナップ　c．ピーチ
ケント　d．パイロット製図用インキ　e．400㍉×330㍉
f．1985年　g．グランプリイラストレイテッド　h．摺本好
作

a. ROTHMANS VERSUS MARLBORO b. Magazine
illustration c. Peach kent d. Drawing ink g. GRAND
PRIX ILLUSTRATED h. Kosaku Surimoto

a．エキセルシャー　b．雑誌　c．キャンソン紙　d．ドローイング・インキ　e．364㍉×515㍉　f．1983年　g．毎日新聞社　h．永野清貴　＊ヴィンテージは趣味じゃないけど絵にはなる。

a. EXCELSIOR　b. Magazine illustration　c. Canson paper　d. Drawing ink　g. THE MAINICHI NEWSPAPERS　h. Kiyotaka Nagano　＊I have no taste of vintaged, but this type looks vintage in illustration.

a．CB72＆カストマイズドGB250　b．カタログ　c．クレセントボード No.310　d．リキテックス，鉛筆，カラーインキ（ドクターマーチン）　e．364㍉×515㍉　f．1985年　g．ブライアン・カーティス・モーターサイクルズ　h．佐原輝夫　＊資料としたCB72の写真に合わせて自分のバイクを撮影して合成した。バイクショップ展示。

a. CB72 ＆ CUSTOM-MADE GB250　b. Catalog　c. Crescent board ＃310　d. Liquitex, pencil, and color ink　g. BRYAN CURTIS MOTORCYCLES　h. Telly Sahara　＊CB72 from a reference photo and GB250, my own bike are double-featured. This work has been exhibited at a bikeshop.

a.『どこへ行こうかツーリング』 b.単行本の表紙 c.ク
レセントボード №310 d.ホルベイン、カラーインキ e.
340㎜×260㎜ f.1984年 g.グランプリ出版 h.安田雅
章 ＊本の表紙にしてはバックの色が暗い。

a. WHERE SHALL WE RAMBLE ABOUT b. Book
cover c. Crescent board #310 d. Color ink g.
GRAND PRIX BOOK PUBLISHING CO., LTD. h.
Masaaki Yasuda ＊Background color was rather dark
as the bookcover.

a.ドゥカッティ b.雑誌表紙 c.クレセントボード
№310 d.アクリル e.585㎜×395㎜ f.1984年 g.電
波新聞社 h.青木正明

a. DUCATI b. Magazine cover c. Crescent board #310
d. Acrylic g. DEMPA PUBLICATIONS, INC. h.
Masaaki Aoki

a.『摺本好作のバイクイラストレイテッド』 b.自著書の
カット c.ピーチケント d.三菱ユニ2B鉛筆 e.
200㎜×260㎜ f.1985年 g.CBS・ソニー出版 h.摺本
好作 ＊あったか味を出すために鉛筆を使用。力を入れる
ところ，ぬくところに神経を使った。

a. KOSAKU SURIMOTO'S BIKE ILLUSTRATED b.
Editorial from his portfolio c. Peach kent d. Pencil
g. CBS / SONY PUBLISHING, INC. h. Kosaku Surimoto ＊I used pencils to express a warm atomosphere.
Also was very careful about the part to concentrate, as
well as the one to relax.

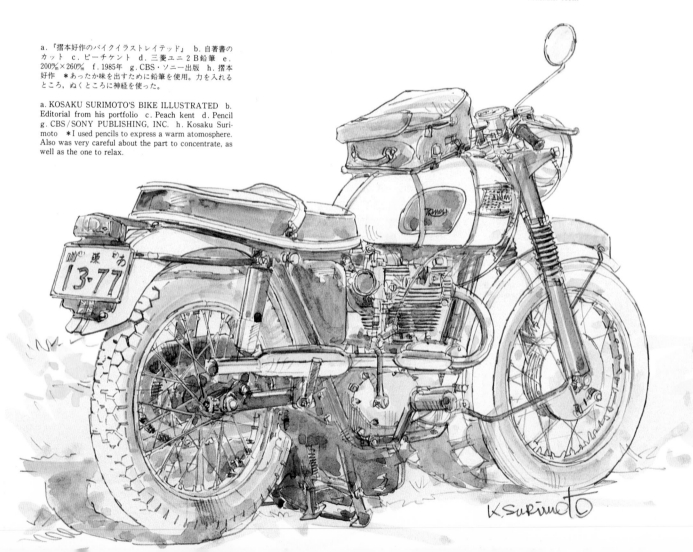

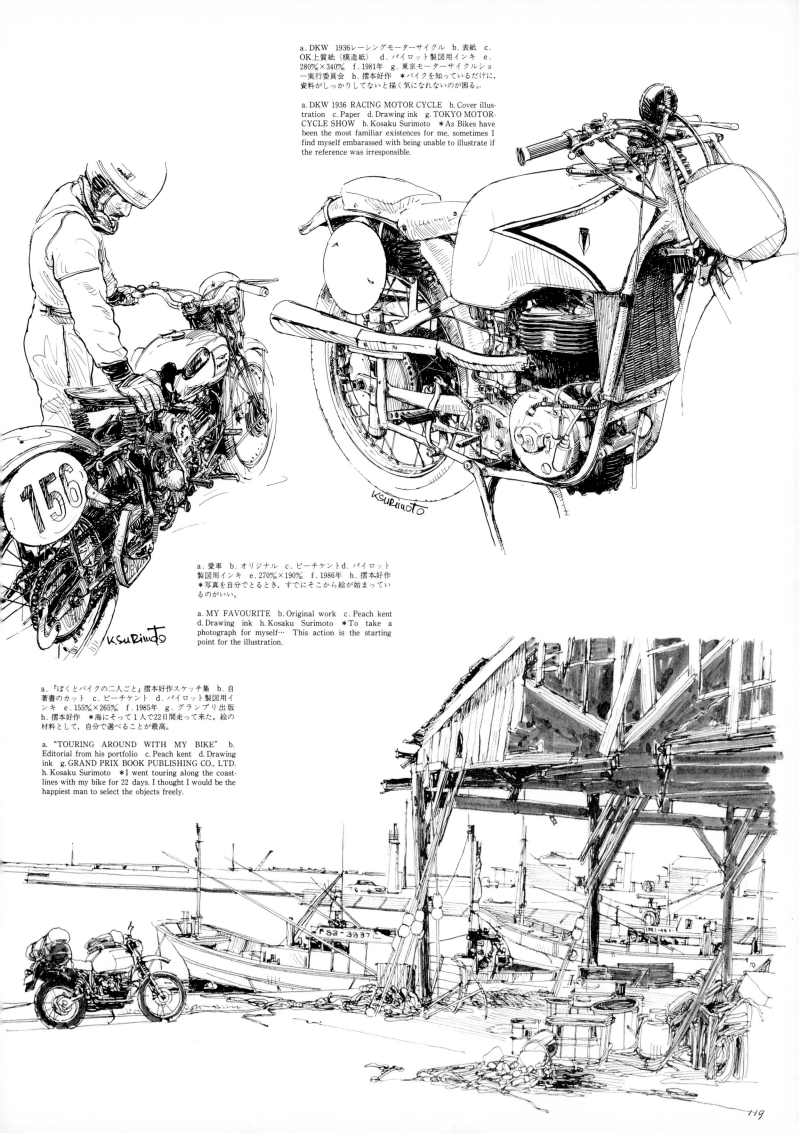

a. DKW 1936レーシングモーターサイクル　b. 表紙　c. OK上質紙（模造紙）　d. パイロット製図用インキ　e. 280㎜×340㎜　f. 1981年　g. 東京モーターサイクルショー実行委員会　h. 摺本好作　＊バイクを知っているだけに、資料がしっかりしてないと描く気になれないのが困る。

a. DKW 1936 RACING MOTOR CYCLE　b. Cover illustration　c. Paper　d. Drawing ink　g. TOKYO MOTOR-CYCLE SHOW　h. Kosaku Surimoto　＊As Bikes have been the most familiar existences for me, sometimes I find myself embarassed with being unable to illustrate if the reference was irresponsible.

a. 愛車　b. オリジナル　c. ピーチケント　d. パイロット製図用インキ　e. 270㎜×190㎜　f. 1986年　h. 摺本好作 ＊写真を自分でとるとき、すでにそこから絵が始まっているのがいい。

a. MY FAVOURITE　b. Original work　c. Peach kent d. Drawing ink　h. Kosaku Surimoto　＊To take a photograph for myself… This action is the starting point for the illustration.

a. 『ぼくとバイクの二人ごと』摺本好作スケッチ集　b. 自著書のカット　c. ピーチケント　d. パイロット製図用インキ　e. 155㎜×265㎜　f. 1985年　g. グランプリ出版　h. 摺本好作　＊海にそって1人で22日間走って来た。絵の材料として、自分で選べることが最高。

a. "TOURING AROUND WITH MY BIKE"　b. Editorial from his portfolio　c. Peach kent　d. Drawing ink　g. GRAND PRIX BOOK PUBLISHING CO., LTD. h. Kosaku Surimoto　＊I went touring along the coastlines with my bike for 22 days. I thought I would be the happiest man to select the objects freely.

レーシング・カー

RACING CARS

a．ポルシェ917-10　b．オリジナル　c．ヴィンセント　ヴェラム　d．マジックカラー，プリスマパステル　e．240㎜×350㎜　f．1979年　h．児玉英雄

a. PORSCHE 917-10　b. Original work　c. Vellum paper
d. Marker and pastel　h. Hideo Kodama

a. フォーミュラ1　b　雑誌『オートスポーツ』ピンナップ
c. クレセントボード No.310　d. リキテックス，鉛筆　e.
230㎜×660㎜　f. 1984年　g. 三栄書房　h. 佐原輝夫
＊コラージュの技法はしばしば使うが，近年のF1は写真が
単調でやりづらい。

a. FORMULA 1　b. Magazine illustration　c. Crescent
board ＃310　d. Liquitex and pencil　g. SANEI SHOBO
PUBLISHING CO.　h. Telly Sahara　＊I often used a
collage techinique on my work. However the recent
photographs of F 1 are taken in a vary monotonous
tone and not so easy to illustrate.

a. ホンダF-1　b. オリジナル　c. ハレパネ　d. リキテッ
クス，ロットリング　e. 350㎜×500㎜　f. 1985年　h. 稲
垣謙治

a. HONDA F-1　b. Original work　c. Panel　d. Liquitex
and rotring pen　h. Kenji Inagaki

a. ブラバム・アルファBT45B　b. オリジナル　c. キャンバスP50　d. 油彩　e. 803㎜×1,163㎜　f. 1985年　h. 牧田哲明　＊ブラバム・フルファに焦点を合わせ，風景に動きを出し，スピード感を表現する。

a. BRABHAM-ALFA BT45B b. Original work c. Canvas d. Oil h. Tetsuaki Makita ＊In this work I tried to forcus the Brabham-Alfa, express the lively background and the speedy feeling, as much as I could.

a. ニューマン　ポルシェ956　b. パッケージ　c. PMパッ
ドイラストレーションボード　d. サインペン, パントンカ
ラーオーバーレイ　e. 364㎜×515㎜　f. 1985年　g. ミツ
ワモデル　h. 中村安広

a. NEWMAN PORSCHE 956　b. Package illustration
c. PM pad illustration board　d. Sign pen and pantone
color overlay　g. MITSUWA MODEL　h. Yasuhiro Nakamura

a. ロスマンズ　ポルシェ956　b. パッケージ　c. PMパッ
ドイラストレーションボード　d. サインペン, パントンカ
ラーオーバーレイ　e. 364㎜×515㎜　f. 1985年　g. ミツ
ワモデル　h. 中村安広

a. ROTHMANS PORSCHE 956　b. Package illustration
c. PM pad illustration board　d. Sign pen and pantone
color overlay　g. MITSUWA MODEL　h. Yasuhiro Nakamura

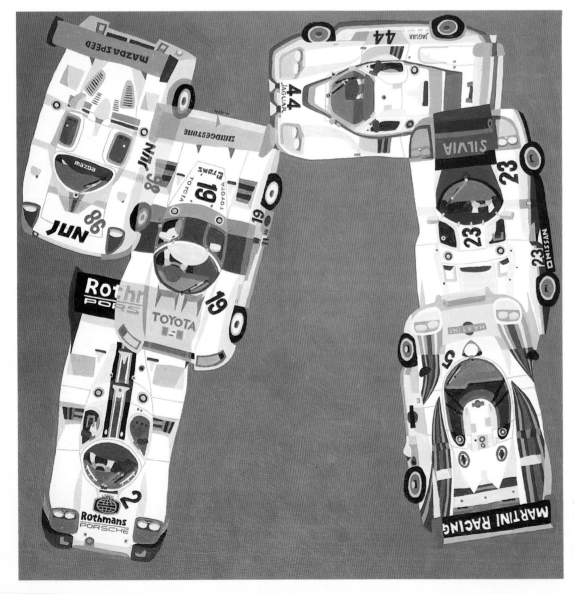

a. WECジャパン'84　b. ポスター　c. B.B.ケント　d. リ
キテックス　e. 515㎜×515㎜　f. 1984年　g. ユート　h.
浅里道晴　＊およその結果を考えながら各車のレイアウト
を考えました。クレームがつきますから。

a. '84 W.E.C. JAPAN　b. Poster　c. B.B. Kent　d. Liquitex　g. UTO CO,. LTD.　h. Michiharu Asari　＊Point
was layout of each car. I should be careful with it, to
avoid claims from clients.

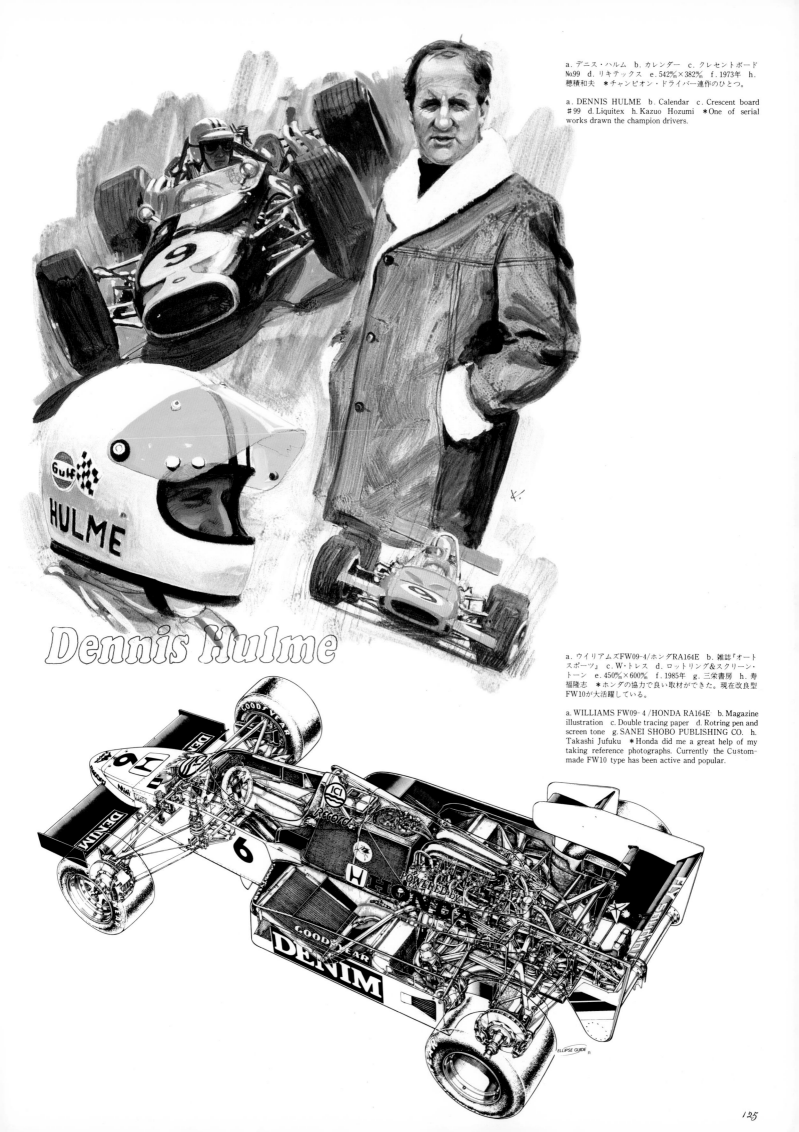

a. デニス・ハルム b. カレンダー c. クレセントボード No.99 d. リキテックス e. 542㎜×382㎜ f. 1973年 h. 穂積和夫 ＊チャンピオン・ドライバー連作のひとつ。

a. DENNIS HULME b. Calendar c. Crescent board #99 d. Liquitex h. Kazuo Hozumi ＊One of serial works drawn the champion drivers.

Dennis Hulme

a. ウイリアムズFW09-4/ホンダRA164E b. 雑誌『オートスポーツ』 c. W・トレス d. ロットリング＆スクリーン・トーン e. 450㎜×600㎜ f. 1985年 g. 三栄書房 h. 寿福隆志 ＊ホンダの協力で良い取材ができた。現在改良型FW10が大活躍している。

a. WILLIAMS FW09-4/HONDA RA164E b. Magazine illustration c. Double tracing paper d. Rotring pen and screen tone g. SANEI SHOBO PUBLISHING CO. h. Takashi Jufuku ＊Honda did me a great help of my taking reference photographs. Currently the Custom-made FW10 type has been active and popular.

a. フェラーリ タイプ125他　b. 雑誌　c. キャンソンケ
ント　d. リキテックス他　e. 305㎜×364㎜　f. 1985年
g. モーターマガジン社　h. 森 優　＊二色という限定さ
れた色数と、モチーフの資料選択に苦労した。

a. FERRARI TYPE 125　b. Editorial for magazine　c.
Canson-Kent　d. Liquitex and mixed media　g. MOTOR
MAGAZINE CO., LTD.　h. Yu Mori　＊I was at pains of
two colors restriction and motif selection,

1948 125 1½litre.

1951 375 4½litre

a. BOB&KAY　b. 雑誌『カー＆ドライバー』　c. キャン
バス　d. リキテックス　e. 530㎜×450㎜　f. 1983年　g.
ダイヤモンド社　h. 小森 誠

a. BOB & KAY　b. Magazine　c. Canvas　d. Liquitex
g. DIAMOND, INC.　h. Makoto Komori

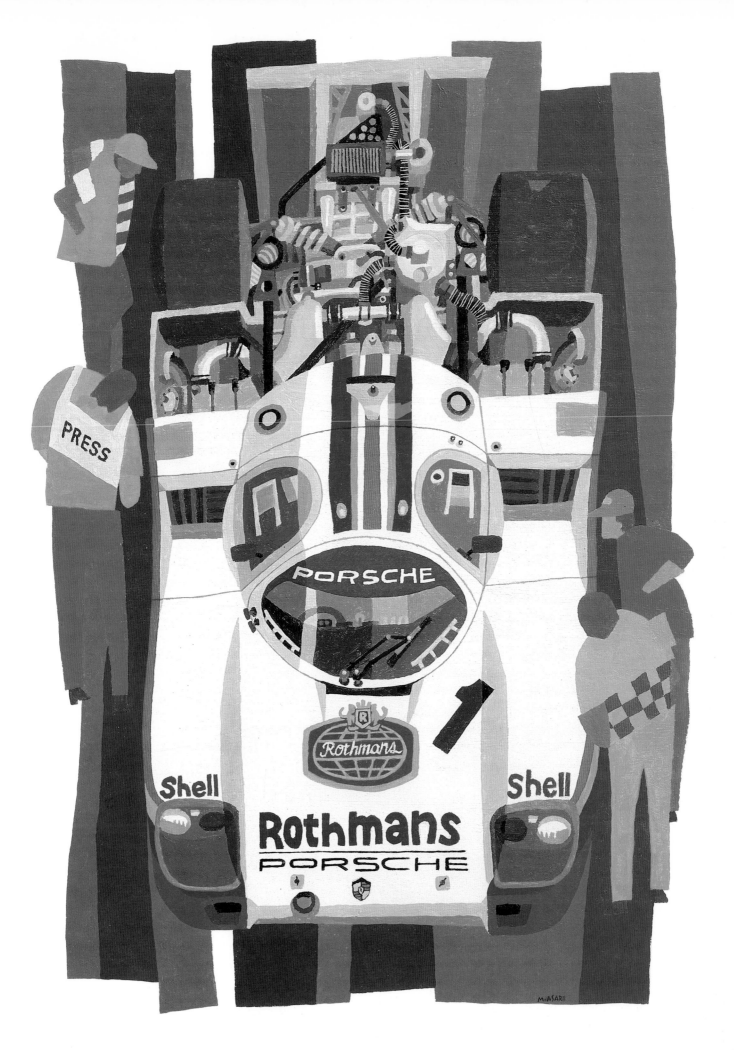

a. ポルシェ956 b. ポスター c. B.B.ケント d. リキテックス e. 594㎜×420㎜ f. 1984年 g. ユート h. 浅里道晴 *実車のNo.1ポルシェのウインドスクリーンは白なんですが，赤にしちゃいました。

a. PORSCHE 956 b. Poster c. B.B. Kent d. Liquitex g. UTO CO., LTD. h. Michiharu Asari *The windscreen of the original was white, but I made it in red.

a. ロータス62　b. オリジナル　c. オリオンプロフェッショナルボード　d. リキテックス　e. 228㍉×400㍉　f. 1984年　h. 榎本竹利　＊JOHN, BOLSTER著によるロータスの専門書の小さなモノクロ写真が参考です。

a. LOTUS 62　b. Original work　c. Orion professional board　d. Liquitex　h. Taketoshi Enomoto　＊Reference source is a small monochrome photograph found out in the book on Lotus, written by John Bolster.

a. レース　b. 絵本　c. クレセントボード No.110　d. リキテックス，ガッシュ　e. 250㍉×260㍉　f. 1984年　g. 小学館　h. 中島　秀　＊レイアウト上，何点かの写真（オートスポーツ誌より）を組合せて作成した。

a. RACE　b. Picture book　c. Crescent board #110　d. Liquitex and gouache　g. SHOGAKUKAN　h. Hide Nakajima　＊I did this work to layout several reference photographs from an automobile magazine.

a. アルファロメオ テーポB b. 雑誌 c. キャンソンケ
ント d. リキテックス他 e. 305㎜×364㎜ f. 1984年
g. モーターマガジン社 h. 森 優 ＊二色という限定さ
れた色数で描くのに苦労したことと、構成をいかにするか。

a. ALFA ROMEO TYPE B b. Editorial for magazine
c. Canson-kent d. Liquitex g. MOTOR MAGAZINE
CO., LTD. h. Yu Mori ＊This work was illustrated
under the restriction on two colors only. That was most
difficult, along with how the best layout should be done.

Alfa Romeo Type B (P3)

Yu. Mori

a. コブラ289 b. 展覧会 c. クレセントボード No.310
d. リキテックス e. 364㎜×515㎜ f. 1983年 h. 佐原輝
夫 ＊JAAAの展覧会用描き下ろし。コブラは最も好きな
クルマのひとつ。

a. COBRA 289 b. Exhibited work c. Crescent board
#310 d. Liquitex h. Telly Sahara ＊This cobra, one
of my most favourite types, has been done for JAAA
Exhibition.

a. デイトナ コブラ クーペ b. 自動車雑誌 c. ケント紙 d. ペンとインキ e. 295㎜×245㎜ f. 1985年 g. 八重洲出版 h. 榎本竹利 ＊好きなクルマを好きなように描かせてもらっているので，楽しい仕事です。

a. DAYTONA COBRA COUPE b. Magazine illustration c. Kent paper d. Pen & ink g. YAESU PUBLISHING CO., LTD. h. Taketoshi Enomoto ＊I am happy to illustrate my favourite car in my farourite style, and this time is the case.

a. パリ・ダカールラリー（岩石） b. カレンダー c. キャンバス d. 油彩 e. 530㎜×727㎜ f. 1984年 g. 三菱自動車工業 h. 牧田哲明 ＊耐久ラリーの厳しさ，自然との戦いに挑むパジェロを迫力ある岩石群を背景に描く。

a. PARIS DAKAR RALLY （ROCKS） b. Calendar c. Canvas d. Oil g. MITSUBISHI MOTORS CO., LTD. h. Tetsuaki Makita ＊Basic elements are the severeness of the rally and challenging Pajero, illustrated with their background as the stern gorges.

a. アウディ　クアトロ　b. 展覧会用　c. クレセントボー
ド No300　d. リキテックス　e. 728㍉×515㍉　f. 1984年
h. 海勢頭清治

a. AUDI QUATTRO　b. Exhibition　c. Crescent board
#300　d. Liquitex　h. Seiji Kaisedo

a. ランチア物語　b. 雑誌タイトル・バック　c. クレセン
トボード No100　d. リキテックス　e. 400㍉×400㍉　f.
1982年　g. 山海堂　h. 細川武志　＊現代的に明るく、あざ
やかになるように心掛けた。

a. LANCIA STORY　b. Title page of magazine　c. Crescent board #100　d. Liquitex　g. SANKAIDO BOOK
PUBLISHING CO., LTD. h. Takeshi Hosokawa　＊I
aimed to draw it as modern, bright, and clear as possible.

a. 国鉄キハ183系特急気動車　b. 図鑑　c. ミューズB.B.
ケント　d. デザイナーズカラー　e. 500㎜×700㎜　f.
1985年　g. 日本交通公社　h. 常味真一　＊北海道へ取材，
寒い中，北斗が走ってくるまで，何時間も待ちました。いい
思い出です。

a. JNR 183 SPECIAL-EXPRESS DIESEL-CAR b.
Pictorial book c. Kent paper d. Designers color g.
JAPAN TRAVEL BUREAU h. Sin'ichi Tsunemi ＊I
went to Hokkaido to see this train. In the cold outside I
waited and watied for his arrival. It has been a good
reminiscence still now.

トレイン

TRAINS

a. 札幌地下鉄6000系　b. 図鑑　c. クレセントボード
No.205　d. デザイナーズカラー　e. 420㎜×600㎜　f.
1985年　g. 日本交通公社　h. 常味真一　＊取材の時に実
車に乗ってみましたが, 電車というよりも, バスに近い感じ
でした。

a. SAPPORO SUBWAY 6000　b. Pictorial book　c. Crescent board　#205　d. Designers　color　g. JAPAN
TRAVEL BUREAU　h. Sin'ichi Tsunemi　＊I actually
got on the rolling stock of this train, but it felt like
rather the one for bus, not for a train at all.

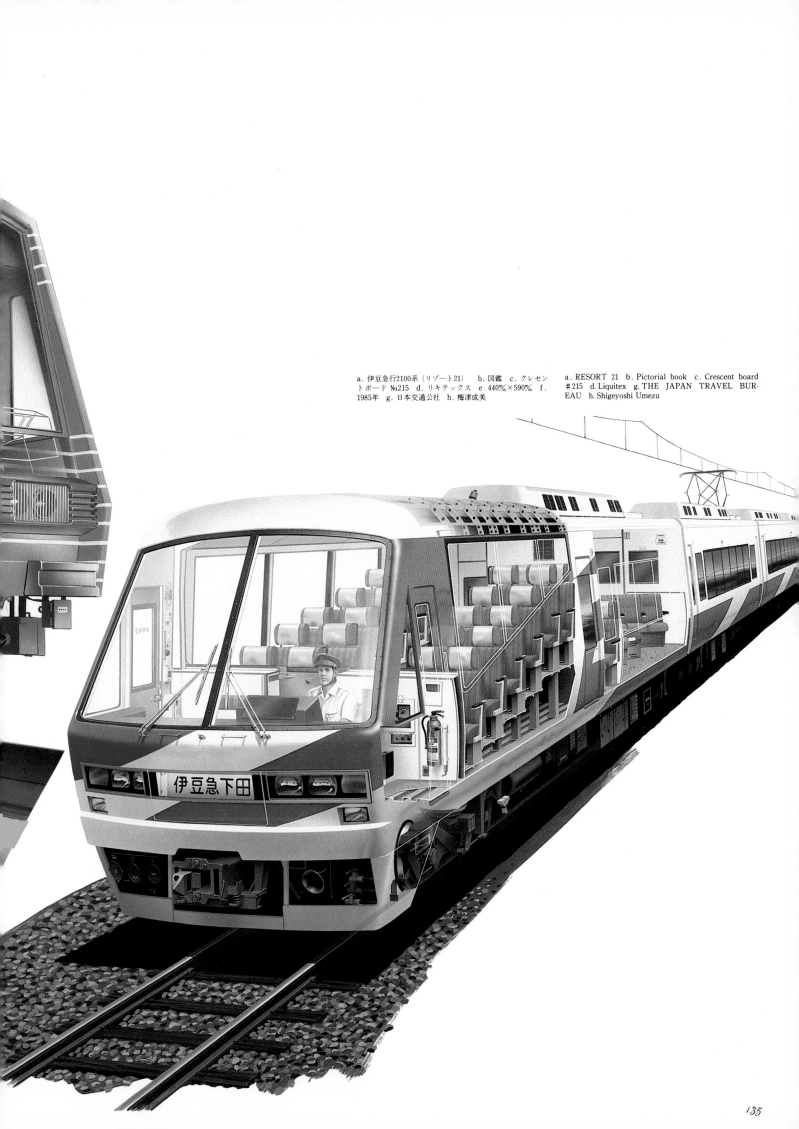

a. 伊豆急行2100系（リゾート21）　b. 図鑑　c. クレセントボード No.215　d. リキテックス　e. 440㍉×590㍉　f. 1985年　g. 日本交通公社　h. 梅津成美

a. RESORT 21　b. Pictorial book　c. Crescent board #215　d. Liquitex　g. THE JAPAN TRAVEL BUREAU　h. Shigeyoshi Umezu

a. DD-51 b. 書籍『日本の鉄道』 c. イラストボード
d. アクリル, ガッシュ e. 300㍉×630㍉ f. 1985年 g.
日本交通公社 h. 鴨下示佳 ＊描く者の目からも取材, 撮
影に参加しました。もっとカットしたかったのですが……。

a. JNR DD-51 b. Book illustration c. Illustration board
d. Acrylic and gouache g. JAPAN TRAVEL BUREAU
h. Tokiyoshi Kamoshita ＊I have joined in taking
photographs and observed it carefully. But I have still
dissatisfied with its realization. Details should be more
simplified.

a. 『私はカンビールになりたい』 b. ポスター c. クレセ
ントボード No.205 d. リキテックス他 e. 595㍉×800㍉
f. 1984年 g. サントリー h. 武田育雄

a. I WANT TO BE A CAN BEER b. Poster c. Crescent board ＃205 d. Liquitex and mixed media g.
SUNTORY LTD. h. Ikuo Takeda

a. JNR EF58電気機関車　b. オリジナル　c. Wトレーシ
ングペーパー　d. ロットリング　e. 365㎜×515㎜　f.
1985年　h. 常味真一　＊日本国有鉄道，全盛時代の電気機
関車です。つばめ，はと，あさかぜなど，を牽引した。

a. JNR EF58 ELECTRIC LOCOMOTIVE　b. Original
work　c. Double tracing paper　d. Rotring pen　h. Sin'
ichi Tsunemi　＊EF58 was enhanced its activity during
the golden days of JNR, hauled numerous passanger
trains.

a. 汽車　b. オリジナル　c. スクラッチボード　d. リキテックス他　e. 230㎜×290㎜　f. 1984年　h. 吉田和弘 ＊Decline of Steamを参考にした。

a. TRAIN　b. Original work　c. Scratch board　d. Liquitex and mixed media　h. Kazuhiro Yoshida　＊Reference source is "DECLINE OF STEAM".

a. ビッグボーイ　b. オリジナル　c. クレセントボード No.310　d. ロットリング　e. 364㎜×515㎜　f. 1986年　h. 相川修一

a. BIG BOY　b. Original work　c. Crescent board ＃310　d. Rotring pen　h. Shuichi Aikawa

a. アメリカチェサピーク & オハイオ鉄道2-6-6-6型　b. オリジナル　c. ワトソンボード　d. ガッシュ, ホルベイン, 透明水彩　e. 380㍉×540㍉　f. 1981年　h. 上田毅八郎　＊戦艦を思わせるマスク。力強い姿。私の最も好きなSLだから比較的楽に描けた。

a. CHEASAPEAKE & OHIO 2-6-6-6'S U.S.A. b. Original work　c. Watson board　d. Gouache and water-color　h. Kihachiro Ueda　＊Front part reminds me of the one for a powerful battleship. Most favourite SL of mine.

a. 無番号SL　b. オリジナル　c. クレセントボード No.99
d. ガッシュ他　e. 290㍉×395㍉　f. 1986年　h. 真田勇夫
＊日本甜菜糖所有。製造所、製作年も出所不明の珍SL。『世界の鉄道'62』（朝日新聞社編）参照。

a. UNTITLED SL TRAIN　b. Original work　c. Crescent board ＃99　d. Gouache and mixed media　h. Isao Sanada　＊The date and place of manufacture are unclear on this quaint SL train. Original art source is from "World Railroad '62" edited by Asahi Newspaper Publishing.

a. 無火機F303　b. オリジナル　c. クレセントボード No.99　d. ガッシュ他　e. 300㍉×430㍉　f. 1986年　h. 真田勇夫　＊旧八幡製鉄で活躍した煙突無しのSL。ボンベの中に蒸気をためている。『世界の鉄道'62』参照。

a. F303　b. Original work　c. Crescent board ＃99　d. Gouache　h. Isao Sanada　＊The old SL train without smokestacks who used to be active in the iron industry. Steam was saved inside a cylinder. Also from "World Railroad '62".

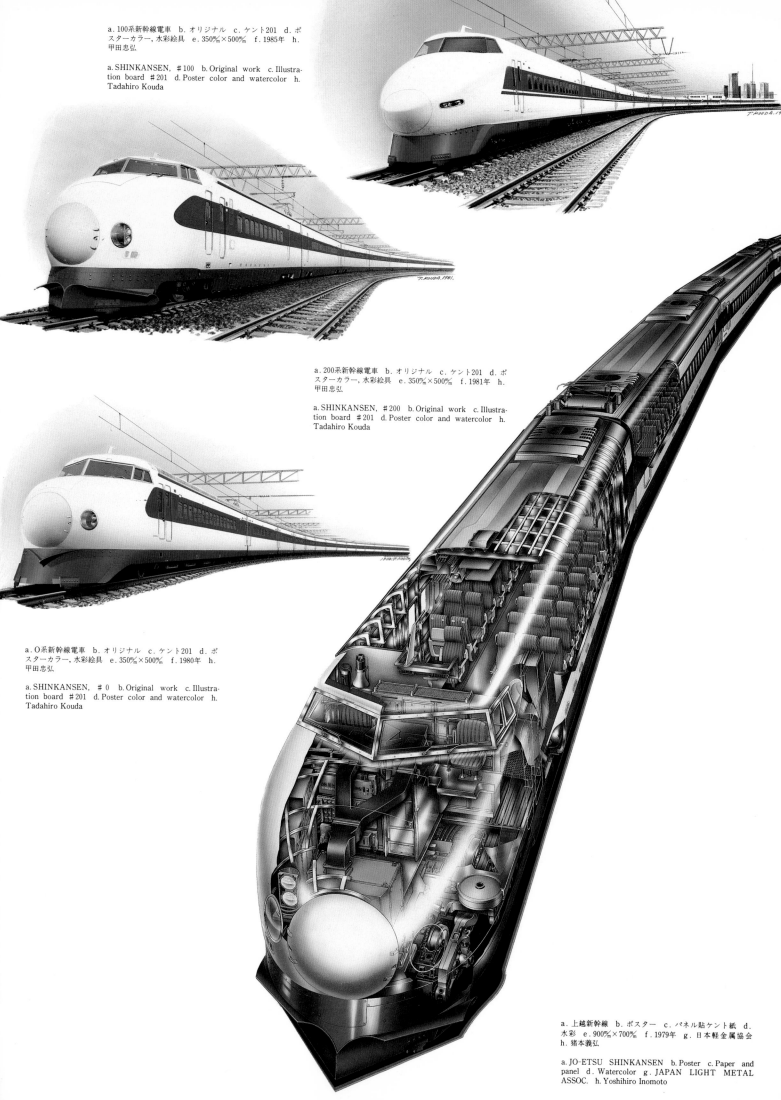

a. 100系新幹線電車　b. オリジナル　c. ケント201　d. ポスターカラー，水彩絵具　e. 350㍉×500㍉　f. 1985年　h. 甲田忠弘

a. SHINKANSEN, #100　b. Original work　c. Illustration board #201　d. Poster color and watercolor　h. Tadahiro Kouda

a. 200系新幹線電車　b. オリジナル　c. ケント201　d. ポスターカラー，水彩絵具　e. 350㍉×500㍉　f. 1981年　h. 甲田忠弘

a. SHINKANSEN, #200　b. Original work　c. Illustration board #201　d. Poster color and watercolor　h. Tadahiro Kouda

a. O系新幹線電車　b. オリジナル　c. ケント201　d. ポスターカラー，水彩絵具　e. 350㍉×500㍉　f. 1980年　h. 甲田忠弘

a. SHINKANSEN, #0　b. Original work　c. Illustration board #201　d. Poster color and watercolor　h. Tadahiro Kouda

a. 上越新幹線　b. ポスター　c. パネル貼ケント紙　d. 水彩　e. 900㍉×700㍉　f. 1979年　g. 日本軽金属協会　h. 猪本義弘

a. JO-ETSU SHINKANSEN　b. Poster　c. Paper and panel　d. Watercolor　g. JAPAN LIGHT METAL ASSOC.　h. Yoshihiro Inomoto

a. Pz.Sf 1.V　b. 雑誌　c. ケント紙　d. アクリル　e.
320㎜×520㎜　f. 1977年　g. 潮書房　h. 高荷義之

a. Pz.Sf 1 . V　b. Magazine illustration　c. Kent paper
d. Acrylic　g. USHIO SHOBO PUBLISHING CO., LTD.
h. Yoshiyuki Takani

タンク & スペシャル

ARMAMENTS

a. パンサー b. パッケージ c. イラストボード d. ア
クリル e. 360㍉×480㍉ f. 1982年 g. ツクダホビー
h. 高荷義之

a. PANTHER b. Package illustration c. Illustration
board d. Acrylic g. TSUKUDA HOBBY CO., LTD.
h. Yoshiyuki Takani

a. バルジの戦い　b. 雑誌口絵　c. キャンバス　d. リキ
テックス　e. 517㎜×640㎜　f. 1974年　g. 婦人画報社
h. 穂積和夫　＊いわゆるバルジ大作戦。折からの雪をつい
てバストーニュ救援に向かうパットン戦車軍団。

a. BATTLE OF THE BULGE　b. Editorial for magazine
Hozumi　＊At the Battle of the Bulge, the illustrated
Patton troops were going to rescue Bastogne.

a. 韓国戦車XK-1　b. 新聞紙面　c. トレーシングペーパ
ー　d. 墨汁，丸ペン，ロットリング　e. 230㎜×364㎜　f.
1984年　g. 大阪新聞社　h. 出射忠明

a. KOREAN TANK XK-1　b. Editorial for newspaper
c. Tracing paper d. Indian ink, pen, rotring pen g.
OSAKA SHINBUN　h. Tadaaki Idei

a. 九七式中戦車　b. パッケージ　c. イラストボード　d. アクリル　e. 350㍉×510㍉　f. 1984年　g. ツクダホビー　h. 高荷義之

a. MIDGET TANK TYPE 97　b. Package illustration c. Illustration board　d. Acrylic　g. TSUKUDA HOBBY CO., LTD.　h. Yoshiyuki Takani

a. 小松ブル D455A　b. JAAA作品展　c. キャンソンボード（荒目）　d. ポスターカラー他　e. 510㎜×720㎜　f. 1984年　h. 真田勇夫　＊巨大なブルほど男性的な迫力を持つものは他には無いだろう。小松のカタログ参考。

a. KOMATSU D455A　b. Exhibited work　c. Canson board　d. Postercolor　h. Isao Sanada　＊There is no such vehicles of strong appeal as a bulldozer. This work was illustrated from a manufacture's catalog.

a. 1943フェデラル　b. JAAA作品展　c. カラーボード（黄色）　d. ポスターカラー他　e. 510㎜×720㎜　f. 1985年　g. 真田勇夫　h.　＊山形県の山奥で、ダム工事に使用された4駆トレーラートラック。日通のマークがある。

a. 1943 FEDERAL　b. Exhibited work　c. Color board (canary yellow)　d. Poster color　h. Isao Sanada　＊A trailer-truck with four-wheel drive which has been used for building a dum deep in a mountain. Here shows logotype of Nippon Tsuun Co.

a. トレーラー　b. レコードジャケット　c. コンピュータ・グラフィックス　f. 1985年　g. RVC　h. 岡本　博

a. TRAILER　b. Record jacket　c. Computer graphics
g. RVC CORPORATION　h. Hiroshi Okamoto

a. マイレッジ-マラソン出場車　b. 1985年JAAA展　c. クレセントボード　d. リキテックス　e. 235㎜×270㎜　f. 1984年　g. チーム　トマト-ジャム　h. 鬼武龍一　＊当社のイラストレーター兼"JAM-DESIGN"代表, 賀川邦彦氏設計製作の車。

a. MILEAGE MARATHON CAR　b. For exhibition　c. Crescent board　d. Liquitex　g. TEAM TOMATO-JAM　h. Ryuichi Onitake　＊This car was planned and produced by Mr. Kunihiko Kagawa, staff illustrator and the representative of the Jam-Design (design studio).

a. マイレッジ-マラソン出場車　b. 1985年JAAA展　c. クレセントボード　d. リキテックス　e. 210㎜×290㎜　f. 1984年　g. チーム　トマト-ジャム　h. 鬼武龍一　＊GOOD-DESIGNの空力ボディ。スタイル賞受賞。ヘルメットもボディの一部。

a. MILEAGE MARATHON CAR　b. For exhibition　c. Crescent board　d. Liquitex　g. TEAM TOMATO-JAM　h. Ryuichi Onitake　＊With the well-designed aerodynamic body, it won a prize of style. The helmet is also a part of its body.

a．クレーン車　b．ポスター　c．クレセントボード No.210
d．リキテックス　e．650㎜×1,000㎜　f．1985年　g．タダ
ノ　h．石崎康秀

a．CRANE CAR　b．Poster　c．Crescent board ＃210　d．
Liquitex　g．TADANO　h．Yasuhide Ishizaki

a．高速用国鉄バス　b．図鑑　c．ケント紙　d．水彩絵具
e．420㎜×590㎜　f．1976年　g．旺文社　h．加地茂裕　＊
夜，透視図法で実物から採寸を行ったので色が暗くなって
しまった。

a．HIGHWAY BUS　b．Pictorial book　c．Kent paper
d．Watercolor　g．OBUNSHA CO., LTD.　h．Shigehiro
Kaji　＊One of my perspective renderings. As the object
was measured at night, color was rather dark.

a. フォード ピックアップ b. リトグラフ集『イーストア
ルバム』 c. B・F・Kリーブス紙 d. リトグラフ e.
478㍉×673㍉ f. 1984年 h. 鈴木英人

a. FORD PICKUP b. Portfolio c. B.F.K. Leaves paper
d. Lithograph h. Eizin Suzuki

a. トヨタ ハイラックス b. 月刊紙の表紙 c. クレセン
トボード No.300 d. リキテックス e. 475㍉×364㍉ f.
1984年 g. JAF出版社 h. 森 優 ＊アイディアの勝負。
バックの部分はエアブラシによる表現。

a. TOYOTA HILUX b. Magazine cover c. Crescent
board #300 d. Liquitex g. JAF PUBLISHING CO.,
LTD. h. Yu Mori ＊This work was a fruit of my ideas.
On background I used airbrush.

a. ジープ b. JAAA展 c. クレセントボード No.115 d.
リキテックス e. 1030㍉×750㍉ f. 1983年 h. 中村
信 ＊ロサンゼルス郊外，海浜の明るい雰囲気を出したか
った。

a. JEEP b. Exhibited work c. Crescent board #115
d. Liquitex h. Shin Nakamura ＊I intended to express
an bright atmosphere of the seashore in Los Angeles
suburbs.

a. スズキLT-4WD　b. カタログ，ポスター　c. クレセントボード №110　d. リキテックス，ガッシュ　e. 520㎜×700㎜　f. 1984年　g. スズキ自動車工業　h. 中島秀　＊実車の完成前からの製作の為，途中設計変更の多いのには閉口した。

a. SUZUKI LT-4WD　b. Catalog and poster　c. Crescent board ＃110　d. Liquitex and gouache　g. SUZUKI MOTOR CORPORATION　h. Hide nakajima　＊I started to draw it before the real model had completed. However the changes of planning was so frequent I was fully stumped them.

a. ダットサントラック　b. オリジナル　c. キャンソン紙　d. アクリル絵具他　e. 350㎜×450㎜　f. 1985年　h. 井川友晴

a. DATSUN PICK-UP　b. Original work　c. Canson paper　d. Acrylic, etc.　h. Tomoharu Ikawa

a. オフロードラン　b. オリジナル　c. クレセントボード No.310　d. ホルベイン カラーインク　e. 330㍉×250㍉ f. 1984年　h. 安田雅章　＊4WDに凝り始めた頃で「こんなの欲しいな，欲しいな」と思いつつ描いていた。

a. OFF-ROAD RUN　b. Original work　c. Crescent board #310　d. Drawing ink　h. Masaaki Yasuda　＊This work was done when I was crazy about 4 WD. So I drew it while thinking this was it.

イラストレーション　ザ・ビークル
ILLUSTRATED TRANSPORTATION

作家索引
INDEX

相川修一
SHUICHI AIKAWA
P.25／P.28／P.62／P.138

1947年＝北海道小樽市に生まれる。1965年＝青山デザイン専門学校卒業。1971年＝セールスプロモーションハウス設立時より参加。1976年＝フリーとなる。1984年＝JAAA入会。現在に至る。著書＝「自動車スタイル変遷図鑑」（グランプリ出版）、「図解ベストドライビング」（グランプリ出版）。
連絡先＝〒142　東京都品川区旗の台 5−22−6
☎ 03(781)1324
＊技術的なことに関しては、ただいま勉強中ですが、技術・方法を問わず、はやく自分なりの世界が表現できるようになりたいと思っています。

Addr : 5-22-6 Hatanodai, Shinagawa-ku, Tokyo 142
Tel : 03(781)1324
＊ I am at the moment studying technical related fields. Regardless of the technical method, I hope to soon be able to make it my own world expressing in my way.

青木正明
MASAAKI AOKI
P.63／P.94／P.95／P.118

1958年＝北海道紋別郡に生まれる。1977年＝北海道紋別北高等学校卒業。1980年＝フリーになり現在に至る。
連絡先＝〒160　東京都新宿区四谷 4−25　マンション新宿御苑603
☎ 03(350)1789
＊最近、ニューヨークに行って、イエローキャブの鮮やかな黄色のボディと、人種や老若、貧富をこえ、そして夢も恋も犯罪も人生の喜怒哀楽までも乗せて走る姿に感動した。思えば札幌で過ごした幼稚園時代からタクシーの運転手は、私にとって憧れの職業だった。将来は、イエローキャブとニューヨークの街や人をテーマにした絵を大画面に描いていこうと思っている。

Addr : # 603 Mansion Shinjuku Gyoen 4-25 Yotsuya, Shinjuku-ku, Tokyo 160
Tel : 03(350)1789
＊ On my recent visit to New York I was deeply moved by the bright yellow bodies of yellow cabs and their dashing figures who without regard to race, young and old, rich and poor, transported dreams, love, guilt as well as the joy, anger, sorrow, and happiness of life in their cabs. Thinking back, I have always wanted to be a taxi driver since my kindergarten days in Sapporo. In the future I want to draw large scenes picturing the theme of yellow cabs and the sights and people of New York.

浅里道晴
MICHIHARU ASARI
P.124／P.127

1953年＝山口県宇部市に生まれる。1973年＝フリーとして雑誌、装画、ポスター等、主に自動車とオートバイ。JAAA会員。
連絡先＝〒177　東京都練馬区石神井町 3−25−8　石神井マンション404
☎ 03(995)8226
＊ピカソ！　マチス！　クレー！　最高だなぁ。写真みたいに描くのは好きではありませんので、3人の大大大先輩（失礼かな？）みたいに車やオートバイの絵を描きたいなぁ。絵はやっぱり絵らしいほうが好きですね。

Addr : # 404 Shakujii Mansion 3-25-8 Shakujii-cho, Nerima-ku, Tokyo 177
Tel : 03(995)8226
＊ Picasso！ Matisse！ Klee！ They're fantastic！ I hate to draw pictures that look like photographs. I want to draw cars and motorcycles like the three great, great masters. I prefer drawings that look like drawings.

井川友晴
TOMOHARU IKAWA
P.58／P.100／P.151

1947年＝大阪市に生まれる。1967年＝大阪デザイナー学院卒業。1973年＝フリーとなる。JAAA会員。
連絡先＝〒550　大阪府大阪市西区江戸堀 1−1−9　日宝肥後橋ビル302号
☎ 06(443)3760
＊乗物に興味を持ち始めたのは、中学の頃、車が曲線の時代だった。メリヤス工場の工員が昼休みにホンダのカブで必死にウイリーの練習をしていたのを思い出す。デザイン学校の時に、ボブ・ピーク、バーニー・フックス、ケン・ダリソンなどのイラストを見て、刺激を受け、イラスト（特に車など）を描く様になりました。

Addr : # 302 Nippohigobashi Bldg. 1-1-9 Edobori, Nishi-ku, Osaka 550
Tel : 06(443)3760
＊ I first developed an interest in vehicles during my junior high school days when the body lines of cars were curves. I remember the factory workers at the knitting mill fervently practicing Wheelies on the Honda "Cub" during their lunch hour break. Upon seeing the illustrations of Bob Peak, Bernie Fuchs and Kenneth Dallison at design school and greatly inspired by them I became an illustrator myself (specializing in cars, etc.).

池松　均
HITOSHI IKEMATSU
P.12／P.16／P.21／P.39

1938年＝東京に生まれる。グラフィック・アートと絵画の勉強のかたわら、意匠・商標法の研究のため日本大学法律学科に入学。宇宙・航空・海洋・歴史・ハード SF などの分野を制作、現在に至る。1978年＝NASAの研究施設への立入り許可を受ける。日本宇宙航空環境医学会々員。日本海洋学会々員。
連絡先＝〒173　東京都板橋区大谷口北町34−5
☎ 03(958)1120
＊第一次、第二次大戦時の飛行機や船を描き続け、開発初期のシャトルに初対面してからその後、ずっと宇宙開発や宇宙科学また、メカ物を絵にしていますが、やはり布を張った複葉機がいつも脳裏に浮かびます。きっといちばん人間的な乗り物なのでしょう。そんなメカの生きた味をもっと表現できたらと、いつも思っています。説明する程の特別な技術はありません。常に新しがらず、あるがままに描く、私はこれが全てです。

Addr : 34-5 Oyaguchi Kitamachi Itabashi-ku, Tokyo 173
Tel : 03(958)1120
＊ I have been deawing World War I and II airplanes and ships and since first seeing the shuttle in its early developmental stages and after that I have been depicting space development and space science as well as mechanical objects. Although doing so, the biplane with canvas wings has always remained in the back of my mind. It is probably the only real human-like plane. I always think about ways to express the feeling of the machines better when they were active in their glorious days. There is no special technique I use which requires explanation. Rather than seeking new things, I draw things as they are. This is everything to me.

石崎康秀
YASUHIDE ISHIZAKI
P.86／P.90／P.149

1940年＝東京で生まれる。1965年＝日本デザインセンター入社。1975年＝フリーとなる。1979年＝JAAA入会。
連絡先＝〒150　東京都渋谷区道玄坂 1−15−3　プリメーラ620　イラストレーションスタジオイシザキ
☎ 03(462)5360
＊作品制作にあたりいろいろな人々に助けていただき紙面にて御礼申し上げます。作図において特に鬼武龍一氏やスタッフの遠藤厚君、ありがとう。仕事は資料をあつめはじめて1カ月ほどかかります。あきないように仕事を続けることを思っています。

Addr : Illustration Studio Ishizaki # 620 Primera, 1-15-3 Dogenzaka, Shibuya-ku, Tokyo 150
Tel : 03(462)5360
＊ In this space I would like to express my appreciation to the various people who have helped me. Particulary concerning the drawings I want to thank Mr. Ryuichi Onitake and Mr. Atsushi Endo of my staff. It takes about one month including collecting materials for my work. I would like to continue illustrating without losing interest.

石橋謙一
KEN'ICHI ISHIBASHI
P.23／P.29／P.31／P.33

1947年＝福岡県北九州市に生まれる。1971年＝九州産業大学芸術学部卒業。1971年＝凸版印刷に入社。1972年＝イラストレーター野口佐武郎氏に師事。1973年＝フリーとなる。JAAA会員。
連絡先＝〒223　神奈川県横浜市港北区日吉本町2400
☎　044(62)0746
＊子供の頃、米軍の飛行場で見た飛行機達の迫力ある飛行ぶりに強い影響を受け、飛行機の虜になりました。以来航空雑誌や飛行機の模型を収集するようになり、模型の箱に描かれた箱絵の真似事をしている内に絵の道に進んでしまいました。仕事では色々の乗り物を描きますが、やはり好きなのは飛行機が一番です。写真では撮れないような設定で描く事と、考証に間違いがないよう、出来る限り多くの資料を集めるよう心がけています。

Addr : 2400 Hiyoshi Honcho Kohoku-ku, Yokohama 223
Tel : 044(62)0746
＊ In my childhood I was deeply influenced with the impressive flying style of the airplanes I saw at the American airforce base and became captivated by them. From that time on I started collecting aviation magazines and model airplanes. I took my first step on the road to drawing while imitating the box art drawn on the model airplane boxes. My work involves drawing various kinds of vehicles but, of course, my favorite is always the airplane. I try to collect as much data as possible that involves drawing facilities which can not be captured by camera and to avoid misrepresenting historical facts.

出射忠明
TADAAKI IDEI
P.26／P.29／P.44／P.145

1928年＝旧満州国大連生まれ。1952年＝三栄書房入社。美術部長、「モーターファン」編集長を経て1974年退社。以来フリーランスの図解専門エディター兼イラストレーターとして独自の分野を拓く。著書は「自動車メカニズム図鑑」「バイクメカニズム図鑑」「飛行機メカニズム図鑑」「図鑑くるま工学入門」など。なお、他誌を執筆中。JAAA会員。
連絡先＝〒151　東京都渋谷区本町2-3-1　渋谷本町マンション84号
☎　03(320)8788
＊のりもののイラストを描き始めたきっかけは子供の頃、低空で飛びまわる多種類の飛行機に魅せられたからであった。戦後はしばらく虚脱状態が続いたが、アメリカのカラフルな乗用車の群を見て新しい絵心が湧き、もともとのメカ好きから図鑑記事に没頭するようになった。なお、子供の頃は毎日絵ばかり描いていたので親にしかられてばかりいたが、イラストがものになるにつれて次第に小言が減り、後にあやまったのを覚えている。

Addr : # 84 Shibuya Honcho Mansion 2-3-1 Honcho, Shibuya-ku, Tokyo 151
Tel : 03(320)8788
＊ I first got hooked on drawing illustrations of vehicles when I became fascinated with the different kinds of airplanes that used to fly around in the sky at low altitude in my childhood. The postwar lethargy continued for sometime, however, upon seeing the group of colorful American cars, they inspired new pictures in me. Basically fond of mechanical things, I became engrossed in illustration work. As a child, I was frequently scolded by my parents for only drawing pictures everyday. The complaints gradually decreased as it began to amount to illustration work. And I remember they made an apology to me later.

稲垣謙治
KENJI INAGAKI
P.50／P.61／P.122

1946年＝東京生まれ。ホンダランド鈴鹿サーキットに「第2回日本自動車GP」の時に入社。7年後フリーとなる。著書「レーシングカーイラストレーション」。JAAA会員。
連絡先＝〒513　三重県鈴鹿市庄野町3500-1
☎　0593(78)5845
＊のりものイラストを描き始めたキッカケは、ホンダランド鈴鹿サーキット在社時代。自動車レースのポスター用イラストレーションを必要に迫られ描く様になった。リキテックスを初めて使った時の印象は、いまだに忘れられない。ジョージ・バーテルやケン・ダリソンを1日中眺めていたのもその頃である。

Addr : 3500-1 Shono-cho, Suzuka-shi, Mie 513
Tel : 0593(78)5845
＊ I first got involved in drawing vehicle posters when I was forced to do a poster illustration of a car race. At that time I was employed at the Honda Land Suzuka Circuit. I will never forget my impression when I first used Liquitex. It was the time I used to spend the whole day gazing at George Bartell's and Kenneth Dallison's work.

猪本義弘
YOSHIHIRO INOMOTO
P.70／P.73／P.76／P.78
P.83／P.84／P.88／P.141

1932年＝熊本市に生まれる。1952年～1956年＝マツダ(旧東洋工業)株式会社に勤務。1958年～1978年＝日産自動車株式会社。後フリーランスとなる。JAAA会員。現在のクライアントは、C.B.S.Publications。
連絡先＝〒104　東京都中央区佃2-22-6　A1004　〒277　千葉県柏市つくしが丘3-18-13

Addr : Kaneko Enterprises, Inc. 15641 Product Ln, A-10, Hustinton Beach CA. 92649 CBS Publications 1499, Monrovia Ave., Newport Beach CA. 92663 A-1004, 2-2-26, Tsukuda, Chuo-ku, Tokyo 3-18-13, Tsukushigaoka, Kashiwa-shi, Chiba

上田毅八郎
KIHACHIRO UEDA
P.34／P.37／P.41／P.42
P.105／P.139

1920年＝静岡県志太郡藤枝町に生まれる。小学校は静岡市内の学校を卒業以後、俊父と共に建築塗装・自動車塗装を経営する傍ら、艦船・飛行機・自動車・陸上交通車両を趣味として勉強。太平洋戦争中は陸軍船舶砲兵として海上戦闘を数多く体験。それを生かして現在は、海洋船舶関係・海運造船関係、プラモデルの箱絵、カレンダーの絵等を数多く要命を受け作品制作中。JAAA会員。
連絡先＝〒431-32　静岡県浜松市貴平町257番地
☎　0534(34)1540
＊私は幼少の頃より機械的に動く物に興味を覚え、少年より実社会へ出ても勉強・仕事の余暇をみては軍艦、飛行機、自動車、汽車等の絵を描き続けて60年。その間、実社会及び戦争の体験を元に、迫力・質感のある絵が描ける様日夜努力してまいりました。今までに描いた絵は4,000枚以上になりました。これからは、歴史に残る様な乗物のイラストをシリーズ毎に描き、皆様にお役に立つ様頑張ります。同好の士よ友達になって下さい。

Addr : 257 Kihei-cho, Hamamatsu-shi, Shizuoka 431-32
Tel : 0534(34)1540
＊ In my childhood days I remember being interested in mechanical moving objects. Finding some free time between studies when I was a boy and between work even after becoming an adult, I have drawn pictures of battleships, airplanes, cars, steam engines, etc. Meanwhile, I have strived to instill a powerful noble character in my drawings based on my experiences from the war and the real world over these last 60 years. The number of pictures drawn up to now exceed 4,000. Each time I draw a series of illustrations on vehicles, I want to leave something behind that can be of historic significance in the future and use to everyone. I look forward to making friends sharing similar interests.

梅津成美
SHIGEYOSHI UMEZU
P.67／P.135

1952年＝東京都新宿区に生まれる。1976年＝應応義塾大学法学部卒業後、野口佐武郎氏に師事。1979年＝フリーランスのイラストレーターとなる。JAAA会員。
連絡先＝〒157　東京都世田谷区上祖師谷2-27-21-203
☎　03(300)0799
＊ろくな知識もないのですが、ただ何となく機械っぽいものが好きで、のりもの、メカニックの絵を中心にかいています。カタログなどの仕事が多いので正確さを求められ、それに答えるよう努力していますが、それ以上に師である野口佐武郎先生のいう「リンゴも車も同じ」という言葉に従って、機械、のりものといったテーマを超えた造形的な絵がかけるようになりたいと思っています。

Addr : 2-27-21-203 Kamisoshigaya, Setagaya-ku, Tokyo 157
Tel : 03(300)0799
＊ Although not very knowledgeable, I just happen to like mechanical things for no special reason and base my drawings on them. Because most of my work involves catalogs, I seek accuracy and make every effort to meet that demand. Moreover, according to Mr. Saburo Noguchi's words, who is my teacher, that an apple and car are the same, I want to be able to draw formative pictures that have crossed over the themes of machinery and vehicles.

榎本竹利
TAKETOSHI ENOMOTO
P.49／P.59／P.94／P.128
P.130

1951年＝東京都府中市に生まれる。1970年＝モーターワールド社に入社。1974年＝フリーとなる。JAAA発足と同時に入会、現在に至る。『ドライバー』『ラジコンマガジン』等にレギュラー執筆中。
連絡先＝〒183 東京都府中市四谷4−57−21
☎ 0423(65)5578
＊プラモデルを作るのはニガ手、でも乗り物が大好き。そんな人が作った乗り物のプラモデルは、接着剤でベトベトしていても、またカラーリングがヘタでも、考証がしっかりしていたり、ヘンなところにこだわっていたりで、楽しいし、何よりも心を打つものがあります。ボクはそんな絵を目指しています。自動車を飼い育てていくうちに、自動車の持つ人間的な温かみが見えてきます。ボクはそれを表現したいのです。

Addr : 4-57-21 Yotsuya, Fuchu-shi, Tokyo 183
Tel : 0423(65)5578
＊ Although he is not very good at making play models, or his constructed play model of a vehicle is sticky with adhesive glue or the coloring is poor, it can be fun when one who love vehicles makes a continuous steady historical study or when he is particular about a certain unusual spot. There is nothing more soul rousing than this, I am for these types of pictures. When you own a car you will start to sense a human-like warmness in the car. This is what I would like to express in my drawings.

大内 誠
MAKOTO OUCHI
P.42／P.92／P.93／P.111
P.112

1949年＝茨城県水戸市生まれ。1970年＝法政大学工学部二部卒業。1968年＝在学中より新宿の印刷会社に4年勤務。後フリーとなる。1977年〜78年＝約1年半に渡り西独ミュンヘン市在住のH.シュレンツィッヒ氏宅に自費留学。後新宿に事務所を開く。JAAA会員。
連絡先＝〒160 東京都新宿区西新宿4−32−6 パークグレース新宿806 エリプスガイド
☎ 03(320)8467
＊幼い頃から車好き。一時は、カーデザイナーを夢見るが、学校の関係で、現在の道へ。小学生時代、夏休みの宿題と称しては、車の透視図を模写して提出する。後に、『カーグラフィック』誌に載るJ.A.アリントン氏の画に魅せられ、星島浩氏に師事を得る。仕事の関係上、ハードなものが多いが、近い内にはソフトなものも描きたい。

Addr : Ellipse Guide # 806 Park Grace Shinjuku 4-32-6 Nishi Shinjuku, Shinjuku-ku, Tokyo 160
Tel : 03(320)8467
＊ I have loved cars since a child and at one time dreamed of being a car designer. However, due to reasons related to school I chose this present vocation. One of my summer vacation homework in grade school was to copy a perspective drawing of a car and present it. Later I became faschinated with an illustration by J.A. Erlington published in Car Graphics magazine and received instructions from Mr. Hiroshi Hoshijima. My work frequently involves hard subjects but recently I would like to try a hand at soft subjects, as well.

岡村栄一
EIICHI OKAMURA
P.89

1954年＝新潟県上越市に生まれる。1976年＝東京デザイナー学院工業デザイン科卒業。1976年＝三栄書房美術部に入社。1986年＝JAAA入会。現在『モーターファン』編集部に在籍中。
連絡先＝〒351 埼玉県和光市下新倉1579
☎ 0484(64)4307
＊自動車の絵を描くきっかけとなったのは、学生時代に読んだ四本和巳氏著『自動車デザイン入門』という本。その中に載っていたデザイン・スケッチの技法、画材に興味をもち、まねごとを始めたのが最初だった。 そして現在もこの技法を使って、クルマのドレスアップや、ニューモデル予想のイラストを描いている。

Addr : 1579 Shimoniikura, Wako-shi, Saitama 351
Tel : 0484(64)4307
＊ I first became intersted in drawing automobiles when I read the book, "An Introduction to Automobile Design" by Mr. Kazumi Yotsumoto during my school days. Fascinated with the techniques of the design sketches and the drawing materials shown in the book, I began to imitate them. That was the first time. I use these techniques even today. My job involves dressing-up cars and drawing illustrations of new model forecasts.

岡本 博
HIROSHI OKAMATO
P.48／P.51／P.56／P.66
P.148

1953年＝愛知県名古屋市生まれ。東京デザイナー学院名古屋校卒業後、1年半イラストレーターに師事。後、上京し『ミスターバイク』の表紙をレギュラーで受ける。1983年＝この頃からコンピュータを使い始める。1984年＝「日経CGグランプリ・アイデア賞」受賞。TVタイトルバック制作、他多数の雑誌表紙を手がける。JAAA会員。
連絡先＝〒150 東京都渋谷区神南1−5−4 ロイヤルパレス原宿404
☎ 03(770)1989
＊以前はそれほどではなかったが、最近、車のことが好きになって来た。しかし、これは一大事なのだ。なぜかと言うと "車にのめり込むと絵がヘタになる" というジンクスがあるからだ。結果、小生は外観だけのノンポリに徹しようと心に強く決めたのだ。その証拠に、足がわりにはゴルフのカブリオレが有り、そして、今年中には新車でコスワース・スーパー7がお遊び車として手に入るのだ。どうだ、どうだぁ〜 カッカッカッ……!!

Addr : # 404 Royal Palace Harajuku1-5-4 Jinnan, Shibuya-ku, Tokyo 150
Tel : 03(770)1989
＊ Although I did not particularly care for cars in the past, I have recently become fond of them. However, this is a matter of consequence. The reason why I say this is because there is a jinx that if you become too engrossed in cars your drawings will be poor. Consequently, I firmly decided I would get pass with a nonpolitical external appearance. So as a proof, I have Golf Cabriolet for business and then, I will get a new car, Cosworth Super 7 to play around with this year. Ha ! Ha ! Ha !

岡本三紀夫
MIKIO OKAMOTO
P.46／P.53／P.54／P.55
P.59

1951年＝東京に生まれる。1972年＝桑沢デザイン研究所卒業。1977年＝日本デザインセンター退社。以後フリーとなる。JAAA会員。
連絡先＝〒150 東京都渋谷区宇田川町2−1 渋谷ホームズ921 スタヂオ・プリズム
☎ 03(463)3086
＊高校時代にいたずらで車の絵を描き始めて、もう十何年か過ぎました。その頃はトレスコープもなく烏口さえ知りませんでした。いろいろな材料、道具を知るにつれ、絵の内容も細かさも変わってきて、最近ようやく自分の描きたいものが描けるようになりました。これから先も車の絵、その他、のりものすべてにわたって仕事をしていくと思いますが、今の描き方でいいのか、違う描き方がいいのか当分迷う日が続きそうです。

Addr : Studio Prism # 921 Shibuya Homes 2-1 Udagawa-cho, Shibuya-ku, Tokyo 150
Tel : 03(463)3086
＊ I started drawing cars in high school while fooling around and it has been more than 10 years or so since then. There was no Tracing-scope at that time and I did not even know a drawing pen. Upon learing the various kinds of material and equipment, the details and contents of my drawings have gradually transformed. Recently, I have finally been able to draw the kind of pictures I have always wanted to draw. Hereafter I look forward to working involving drawings of cars while expanding to all other kinds of vehicles, as well. However, I will be probably for a long time wondering whether my present drawing style is good or whether another would be better.

鬼武龍一
RYUICHI ONITAKE
P.113／P.114／P.148

1944年＝東京都世田谷区生まれ。1968年＝東京芸術大学美術学部卒業。1970年＝同大学院鍛金専攻科修了。在学中よりHONDAのテクニカルイラストレーションを手がける。1977年＝TOMATO & DESIGNERS CO., LTD設立。1979年＝JAAA入会。バイク好きのイラスト仲間達と、"TEAM＝TOMATO-JAM" 結成。
連絡先＝〒180 東京都武蔵野市西久保3−4−20−201
☎ 0422(55)0566
＊金属彫刻家を目標として勉強して来たはずなのですが、いつの間にかイラストが本業になってしまいました。マニュアルの仕事から始めたせいか、作図の段階で手を離れる事が大半です。一年中新しい四輪や、バイクのメカニズムに接する事が出来て楽しみなのですが、設計の良く出来た車ほどイラストも完成度の高いものになる様です。20年後の私は、どんなトライアルバイクに乗っているのでしょうか。(多分リタイアしてますね)

Addr : 3-4-20-201 Nishikubo Musashino-shi, Tokyo 180
Tel : 0422(55)0566
＊ I had primarily studied to become a metal sculptor and somewhere along the way illustration became my true profession. Whether it can be attributed to starting off with manual work, a large majority involves hands off in the diagram stage. It is fun to be able to do work concering new car and the mechanical systems of bikes all year round. The better the car is designed, the higher level of perfection my illustrations reaches. After 20 years I wonder what kind of trial bike I will be riding. (Though I will probably be retired.)

小野直宣
NAONOBU ONO
P.74／P.75／P.81／P.91
P.96

1936年＝東京都杉並区に生まれる。1958年＝多摩美術大学図案科卒業。1958年＝日産自動車制作室勤務。1972年＝フリーランス・イラストレーターとなる。自動車、家電、カメラ等、各メーカーのテクニカルイラストを手がけ、カレンダーで通産大臣賞、ポスターで電通賞、新聞広告で朝日広告賞、日経賞等を受賞。
連絡先＝〒168　東京都杉並区高井戸東３－６－15　(有) アトリエ小野
☎ 03(333)9117
＊大学一年の冬、1954年の学期末コンクールで、ダットサン乗用車のポスターを描き、日産自動車の宣伝課に持参し、それがきっかけで、自動車のイラストを描き続ける事になりました。その頃は、カラー写真の色が不安定なせいもあり、カタログは大部分イラストでしたが、その後カラー写真の色が良くなるにつれて、外観のイラストが減少する、反面スケルトンの仕事が多く要求されるようになり、今日に至る。

Addr : Atelier Ono 3-6-15 Takaido Higashi, Suginami-ku, Tokyo 168
Tel : 03(333)9117
＊ In the winter of my freshman year I drew a poster of the Datsun car for the 1954 end of the term competition and took it to the public relations departmant of Nissan Motor Company. This was how I got into car illustrations and have been doing it since then. In those days a large portion of my work involved illustrations for catalogs due to partially the unstable color of color pictures. However, as the color of color pictures later improved, the work load of exterior view illustration decreased. On the other hand, work revolving around skeletons has today grown greatly in demand.

海勢頭清治
SEIJI KAISEDO
P.102／P.106／P.130

1950年＝沖縄県那覇市に生まれる。イラストは独学。1978年＝上京する。1980年＝フリーのイラストレーターとして仕事を始める。JAAA会員。
連絡先＝〒164　東京都中野区中央１－１－12
☎ 03(363)9270
＊小学生の頃は月光仮面、中学の頃は戦艦大和にゼロ戦、高校に上がるとバイクにクルマに女性のヌードとイラストを描いていた。現在も雑誌「ドライバー」の表紙を描いておられる松本秀実氏のイラストを見て、「よし!! 俺もプロのイラストレーターになろう」と思ったが、不良少年から不良青年へと毎日クルマと共に夜遊びばかり、仕事としてイラストを描くようになったのは30歳になってから。最近はカーキチをテーマにして漫画を描くつもりでいる。

Addr : 1-1-12 Chuo, Nakano-ku, Tokyo 164
Tel : 03(363)9270
＊ I drew Gekko Kamen, the Moonlight Rider in grade school, Zero Fighters and the battleship Yamato in junior high school and bikes, cars and nude girls in high school. When I saw the cover of Driver magazine by Mr. Hidemi Matsumoto who is still drawing today, I decided that I could too become a professional illustrator. Moving on from a bratty kid to a juvenile delinquent youth, all I did was to cruise during the day and play at night. I did not really start working until I was 30 years old. Recently, I have plans to draw a cartoon about being car crazy as my theme.

加地茂裕
SHIGEHIRO KAJI
P.22／P.24／P.29／P.112
P.149

1952年＝京都府西陣に生まれる。京建具屋の次男で20歳まで建具の職人修業。学校も伏見工業木材工芸課。72年頃二玄社刊の猪本義弘様の本「オートモービル イラストレーション」を拝見し、ショックを受けて進路変更。製図屋３年、イラスト屋４年修業し独立。1980年～1984年までイラストのみ休業。最近少しづつイラストを描き始めています。JAAA会員。
連絡先＝〒602　京都府京都市上京区今出川通千本東入ル東上善寺町159番地　コーポ峰505号
☎ 075(441)7277
＊陸、海、空、のりものや機械が好きで、ガキの時からいたずら描きばかりしてました。人物には興味が無かったので仕事で描く事はありますがヘタです。これからの目標は尊敬しています、猪本様、大内様のウデマエに少しでも近づく事です。のりもの絵は古典的なオートバイを描きたいです。

Addr : ♯ 505 Corpo Mine, 159 Higashi Jozenji-cho, Imadegawa Dori Sembon Higashi Iru, Kamigyo-ku, Kyoto 602
Tel : 075(441)7277
＊ I love vehicles of the land, sea, air in addition to airplanes and when I was a kid I used to fool around and draw them all the time. Because I am not interested in people, my work dealing with them is not very good. My future goal is to do work like those of Mr. Inomoto and Mr. Ouchi I admire, but that can never be half as great. I hope to draw classical motorcycles in my illustrations of vehicles.

鴨下示佳
TOKIYOSHI KAMOSHITA
P.9／P.30／P.44／P.66
P.68／P.136

1938年＝東京都小金井市に生まれる。日大卒業後パッケージデザインに従事。1967年＝フリーとなりビークルを中心に、図鑑、雑誌、パンフレット、ポスター、パッケージ等に透視図や外観を描いて今日に至る。JAAA会員。東京グラフィックデザイナーズクラブ会員。航空ジャーナリスト協会会員。
連絡先＝〒184　東京都小金井市本町５丁目25－24
☎ 0423(81)6925
＊子供の頃から絵が好きで、特に乗物は良く描きました。それを一生する事になるとはツユ知らず。好きな仕事で生活をしているのですから締め切りを特に強く迫られない限り、どんなに忙しくとも毎日仕事を楽しんでおります。願わくば気に入った仕事を充分な資料でわくわくする様なテーマの絵の割合を多くしたい。

Addr : 5-25-24, Honcho, Koganei-shi, Tokyo 184
Tel : 0423(81)6925
＊ I liked pictures when I was little and especially drew vehicles. I never thought it would become my long life profession, though. Because I am making a living doing the kind of work I love, no matter how busy I am as far as concerning rough deadlines, I enjoy doing my work everyday. If I could have it my way and with the sufficient material, I would like to do a large portion of my picture themes involving some kind of work I like where you could get excited.

小池繁夫
SHIGEO KOIKE
P.10／P.14／P.24／P.25
P.31／P.32

1947年＝新潟県小千谷市に生まれる。1967年＝日本デザインスクール卒業。在学中より新井亮事務所に在籍。1971年＝フリーとなる。
連絡先＝〒167　東京都杉並区善福寺３－19－２
☎ 03(399)3468
＊テクニックのみに寄りかかった絵にならない様に念願しています。

Addr : 3-19-2 Zenpukuji, Suginami-ku, Tokyo 167
Tel : 03(399)3468
＊ I hope that my drawings do not solely depend on technique.

甲田忠弘
TADAHIRO KOUDA
P.141

1935年＝神奈川県横須賀市に生まれる。1953年＝東急車輛製造株式会社に入社。現在車両設計部デザインセンター勤務。
連絡先＝〒236　神奈川県横浜市金沢区釜利谷町1349
☎ 045(784)8718

Addr : 1349 Kamariya-cho, Kanazawa-ku, Yokohama-shi, Kanagawa 236
Tel : 045(784)8718

小谷智昭
TOMOAKI KOTANI
P.61／P.62

1933年＝東京に生まれる。1955年＝文化学院美術科卒業。1957年＝武蔵野美術大学卒業。直後からフリーのイラストレーターとして制作を続ける。一時期は請われて自動車月刊誌の編集長を勤める。本業は洋画（アプストラクト）で、日本美術家連盟に所属している。イラストは主に新車予想スタイリングを視覚化するのを得意としている。JAAA会員。
連絡先＝〒121 東京都足立区花畑5－6－3－402
☎ 03(884)8042
＊のりものに限らずイラストを描きたいと思った動機は、終戦直後に見たアメリカの雑誌『ルック』『コリヤーズ』『サタディイブニングポスト』『ポピュラーサイエンス』『エイビアション』などの作品に感動したのが始まりのようだ。イラストという言葉が日本に定着していない頃、サインにILLUSTRATEDと書いて、編集者に「コレは何ですか?」と問われたのを懐かしく想いだす。ヨーロッパではイラストレーターでは意味が通じなかった。

Addr : 5-6-3-402 Hanabatake, Adachi-ku, Tokyo 121
Tel : 03(884)8042
＊ The time that led me to think I would like illustrating various subjects, not only limited to vehicles, was soon after the war. I was very much moved by the works I saw in the American magazines—— "Look", "Colliers" "Saturday Evening Post", "Popular Science", "Aviation" etc. Before the word, "Illustration" was adopted in Japan, I fondly remember my editor saying, "what's this", when he saw it signed illustrated by Tomoaki Kotani. As a matter of fact, the word, "illustrator", was not understood in Europe.

児玉英雄
HIDEO KODAMA
P.48／P.105／P.121

1944年＝神奈川県横浜市に生まれる。1966年＝多摩美術大学デザイン科卒業。1966年＝西ドイツ、アダム・オペル自動車会社に入社。自動車雑誌『CAR GRAPHIC』『NAVI』に寄稿。JAAA会員。
連絡先＝〒 AM HUHLCHEN 7 A, 6500 MAINZ, WEST GERMANY
☎ (06131)832939
＊子供の頃から好きだった車が、毎日の仕事となり、新型車のデザイン開発にたづさわる一方、これもまた好きな自動車の絵も時折り息抜きに描く様になった。特に古い車を描いていると、思わぬ処に、気がつかなかった面や線の構成があったりしてなかなか楽しいものです。

Addr : AM Huhlchen 7A, 6500Mainz, West Germany
Tel : (06131)832939
＊ Cars which I have ever loved since childhood have become my daily fare of work now where I am involved in the design development of new car models. Meanwhile, I sometimes do that or draw picturers of cars as a form of relaxation. Particularly when I draw old cars, it is quite enjoyable from the aspect where you can be carefree without thinking and the structure of lines are there.

小森 誠
MAKOTO KOMORI
P.57／P.60／P.126

1949年＝京都府綾部市に生まれる。1969年＝大阪デザイナー学院卒業。1970年＝アドプロに入社。1971年＝フリーとなる。JAAA会員。
連絡先＝〒107 東京都港区南青山5－6－16 第1中島ビル3F 小森イラストレーション
☎ 03(407)1224
＊まず最初に車があって、日夜、車だけを描き続けていた頃がありまして、描き続けているうちに、車を囲んでいる空気の様な物を描きたくなってきまして、このあたりから映画っぽくドラマチックな演出なんかシカケてみたり、そんな風に車だけを描くよりも、車を中心としたシカケの方に気分が働く様になって来るのです。

Addr : Komori Illustration 3rd Fl., First Nakajima Bldg, 5-6-16 Minami Aoyama, Minato-ku, Tokyo 107
Tel : 03(407)1224
＊ First I only drew cars night and day. Soon I felt like drawing things like the atmosphere that enveloped cars. From then I looked for some kind of device that could present a dramatic, movie-like atmosphere. In this way, my mind started to work on how to capture the soul of the car rather than just the car itself.

斉藤 信
SHIN SAITO
P.81

1949年＝青森県生まれ。高校卒業後上京。デザイナーからイラストレーターに転身。JAAA会員。
連絡先＝〒229 神奈川県相模原市上溝6－13－9
☎ 0427(22)2562

Addr : 6-13-9, Kamimizo, Sagamihara-shi, Kanagawa 229
Tel : 0427(22)2562

斎藤 寿
HISASHI SAITO
P.100／P.102／P.104／P.106

1936年＝青森県弘前市生まれ。1954年＝青森県弘前高校卒業。1960年＝フリーになる。JAAA会員。
連絡先＝〒220-02 神奈川県津久井郡津久井町太井442－4
☎ 0427(84)5214
＊家業が運送店のせいか、自動車という物が常に生活の一部となって成長して来ました。中学生の頃からほとんどの時間絵を描いて過ごし、オートバイ、ドリームカーなどの設計? もスケッチ・ブックの中にたくさん残って居ます。当時はこれが生活の手段になるとは思ってもみませんでした。車そのものを描くより、その車が置かれている場を感じさせる絵にしたいと思っています。

Addr : 442-4 Ooi, Tsukui-cho, Tsukui-gun, Kanagawa 220-02
Tel : 0427(84)5214
＊ Whether it was due to the fact that our family was in the freight business, I grew up with things like cars and trucks as a constant part of my life. In junior high school days I spent most of my time drawing and my sketchbooks remain filled with designs(?) of motorcycles and dream cars. I never thought at that time it would become a means of livelihood for me. Rather just drawing cars I want to draw pictures of places where you can feel the car.

坂口 学
MANABU SAKAGUCHI
P.94

1960年＝東京都港区生まれ。大阪外国語大学フランス語科中退。JAAA会員。
連絡先＝〒160 東京都新宿区新宿5－11－18 ライオンズマンション605
☎ 03(356)4108
＊午後、いつもより少し早めにオフィスを出る。アスファルトの上に落ちた植え込みのシルエットがすっかり長くなっている。手の中でキーをおもちゃにしながら駐車場を愛車へと歩く。少し歩いて立ち止まり、煙草に火をつけた。両目だけはしっかりと愛車を見つめながら——。車好きなら似たような経験はありませんか? モチーフを単にリアルに描くだけではなく、そんな情感までも伝われば、と思っています。

Addr : # 605 Lions Mansion, 5-11-18 Shinjuku, Shinjuku-ku, Tokyo 160
Tel : 03(356)4108
＊ In the afternoon I leave the office a little earlier than usual. The silhouette of the bushes falling over the asphalt has already gotten longer. Playing with the key in my hand I walk over to my beloved car in the parking lot. Walking a little ways, I pause, light my cigarette and smoke as my eyes gaze over the car. Have you ever experienced a love like this for a car? More than just merely drawing a real representation of the motif I will try to convey the feelings, as well.

佐竹政夫
MASAO SATAKE
P.20／P.22／P.33／P.98

1949年＝千葉県船橋市に生れる。1969年＝関口猪一郎氏に師事。以後フリーのイラストレーターとしてプラモデル各社のパッケージアートを手掛けている。JAAA会員。航空ジャーナリスト協会々員。趣味は航空機模型製作。最近念願のクラリネットを手に入れ，御近所のひんしゅくをかっている。
連絡先＝〒270　千葉県松戸市常盤平４－４－１　ビューグリーン504号
☎　0473（86）7370
＊子供の頃からのプラモデルマニアがこうじてイラストレーターに成ってしまった。中でもヒコーキ，飛ぶ物ならジェットからブーメランまで好き。一時はハンググライダーを駆って毎週飛び回っていたのだが，最近はそれも休業中。しかし，その体感を描き込めたらと思うのだが……。

Addr : # 504 View Green 4-4-I Tokiwadaira, Matsudo-shi, Chiba 270
Tel : 0473(86)7370
＊ The play model manuals of my childhood days have developed into an illustrator. Among airplanes and flying objects I like jets and boomerangs. For a while I flew a hang glider every week. Although I have recently stopped I would like to inspire that sensation into my drawings.

真田勇夫
ISAO SANADA
P.140／P.147

1933年＝青森県青森市生まれ。1952年＝山形県鶴岡南高校卒。1952年＝伊藤オフセット印刷入社。1958年＝モーターファン入社。1959年＝フリーとなり，主としていすゞ自動車のカタログ制作に従事。JAAA創設と同時に入会。1970年＝広告代理店㈱全広社制作部入社。
連絡先＝〒104　東京都中央区銀座２－６－５　越後屋ビル５Ｆ　㈱全広社
☎　03（567）9591
＊昭和ヒトケタ族なので小学校時代は，野外写生以外は，殆ど飛行機，軍艦，戦車などを描いていた。印刷会社で烏口やカーブ定規の使い方を習い，関を見ては，夢の車を創造して，モーターファン社に投稿し，入社することになった。アメリカの週刊誌の車の広告が殆んどイラストである事に大きなショックを受け，独学で必死にまねて勉強したものです。大好きなクラシックカーを，どんどん描いてゆきたいと思っています。

Addr : Zenkoku Co., Ltd. 5 Fl., Echigoya Bldg. 2-6-5, Chuo-ku, Tokyo 104
Tel : 03(567)9591
＊ Because I am of the early Showa-born generation, I spent most of time drawing airplanes, battle ship, tanks, etc., besides outdoor sketches. I learned to use a drawing pen and curve ruler at a printing company. Later, finding some spare time I created my dream car and submitted it to Motor Fans Co. Which I joined. I was greatly shocked to find out that almost all of the advertisements for cars in American weekly magazines were illustrations. Self-taught, I copied and studied them fervently. In the future I hope to continue drawing my favorite classic cars.

佐原輝夫
TELLY SAHARA
P.28／P.56／P.117／P.122
P.129

1952年＝長野県松本市に生まれる。1971年＝武蔵野美術大学中退後，草思社に入社。1975年＝フリーとなる。多くの自動車雑誌に執筆するほか『ホットドッグプレス』などでファッション，スポーツものを手がける事が多い。JAAA会員。
連絡先＝〒154　東京都世田谷区三軒茶屋１－４１－１４　猪野ビル402号
☎　03（418）8444
＊ラク描き大好き少年が本気になったのは，師と仰ぐ穂積和夫氏著『自動車のイラストレーション』（ダヴィッド社）に触れてから。絵づくりや技法などで大きな影響を受けた。クルマのみを細かく描くよりは，レースやリゾートなど，まわりの雰囲気を伝えるものが好き。特に明るい陽ざし，カラッとした色合いなどを心がけている。

Addr : # 402 Ino Bldg. 1-41-14 Sangenjaya, Setagaya-ku, Tokyo 154
Tel : 03(418)8444
＊ As a boy who loved scribbling, I first became seriously interested when I came into contact with "Illustrations of Automobiles" by Mr. Kazuo Hozumi who I looked up to as my teacher. It was a great influence on my drawing methods and technique. Rather than just drawing cars I like it where atmospheres like races and resorts can be conveyed. I try in particular to present a bright disposition and clear shades of color.

三五英夫
HIDEO SANGO
P.18／P.21／P.98／P.103

1943年＝東京・赤坂生まれ。日本大学芸術学部在学中に東映のTV製作の仕事を始め，中退した後，1967年に独立。グラフィックデザインを約10年経験した。1977年＝フリーのイラストレーターに転じ現在にいたる。雑誌関係とコマーシャルデザインのイラストを主な仕事としている。JAAA会員。
連絡先＝〒162　東京都新宿区市谷田町３－21
☎　03（268）0319
＊仕事でドキュメント物を始めてから，陸，海，空と様々な人物やのりものが題材だが，それにまつわる背景を共に表現しなければならない。車ひとつ描く時も，主題の車が大事なのはもとより，その時代の歴史，文化，人間，その他諸々とかなり広範囲にわたる資料捜しが大変である。最近は今まで蓄積してきた資料を基にSF的発想でものの形，光，影を描くことに専念している。

Addr : 3-21 Ichigaya-Tamachi, Shinjuku-ku, Tokyo 162
Tel : 03(268)0319
＊ Because I was working in the beginning with documentaries, my subject involved land, sea, air along with the various kinds of people and vehicles, as well as their surrounding background. More important than the main theme of the car were the history, culture and the people of that period. It is cumbersome to research all the material on the various other items, as well, that span over a considerable wide range. Recently, I have devoted myself to drawing the shapes, light, and shadows of objects through a SF concept based on all the material accumulated up to now.

嶋岡五郎
GORO SHIMAOKA
P.37／P.110

1936年＝福岡県北九州市に生まれる。1955年＝福岡県小倉高校卒。グラフィックデザイナーとして雑誌社（２社）をふりだしに，デパート宣伝部，デザイン会社などに勤務。1970年＝フリーとなる。1976年頃からイラスト一本の生活に入る。1984年＝JAAA入会
連絡先＝〒357-01　埼玉県飯能市原市場406-１
☎　04297（7）1580
＊男の子は乗り物が好き――。幼少の頃からのメカ好き，のりもの好きで，少年時代のモチーフはもっぱら飛行機，軍艦，戦車，蒸気機関車等々に集中していた。終戦の翌日，グラマン艦載機が２機，校庭に立つ２本の銀杏の間をぬけ校舎の屋根をスレスレに飛び抜けて行った。教室の窓から見たこの一瞬を早速ノートに鉛筆で再現したのは小学校三年の時，疎開地徳島県の一山村での記憶である。あれから40年余，未だに乗り物が好きである。

Addr : 406-1 Haraichiba, Hanno-shi, Saitama 357-01
Tel : 0429(77)1580
＊ Little boys like vehicles. I have always liked mechanical objects since a tot and being fond of vehicles, my motif during grade school focused exclusively on airplanes, battleships, tanks, steam engines, etc. On the next day following the end of the war II Grummans carrierborne aircrafts passed through the two ginkgo trees standing in our schoolyard and sped away over the rooftop of the school building. Watching from my classroom window I immediately grabbed my pencil and tried to capture this instant in my notebook. I was in the 3rd grade then. It is a fond memory of an evacuation site at a mountain village in Tottori Prefecture. It has been about 40 years since then and I am still fond of vehicles.

寿福隆志
TAKASHI JUFUKU
P.108／P.114／P.125

1945年＝鹿児島県鹿児島市生まれ。1967年～1982年＝自動車専門誌の出版社。三栄書房美術部に在籍。1982年＝独立。フリーのイラストレーターとなる。テクニカルイラストレーションの仕事場 "エリプスガイド"（ダ円定規の意）を新宿に開設。1985年＝銀座に仕事場を移転。現在に至る。JAAA会員。
連絡先＝〒104　東京都中央区銀座１－14－４　藤平ビル４Ｆ　エリプスガイド
☎　03（564）6826
＊多くの作家達と同様に私も子供の頃から，のりものと絵を描くことが好きだった。高校生時代にケン・ダリソン，ボブ・ピーク等アメリカのアーティスト達の絵に刺激され，大好きな "車と絵" の結びついた仕事が出来たらと漠然と考えていた。しかし，就職した出版社でその "実際" に接し，憧れでは仕事にならない現実を知らされた。現在は別の形で "車と絵" の世界を仕事にしている。子供の頃から憧れていたのりものと絵の世界は趣味として大切にしたいと思う。

Addr : Ellipse Guide 4 Fl., Fujihira Bldg. 1-14-4 Ginza, Chuo-ku, Tokyo 104
Tel : 03(564)6826
＊ Like many illustrators, I had my beginnings drawing pictures of vehicles in my childhood days. In high school days I was greatly inspired by the drawings of the American illustrators, Ken Dallison and Robert Peak and thought how great it would be to be able to do work connected to automobiles, my favorite topic. However, I have learned the true reality that just the desire for the work was not enough after actually experiencing it through employment at a publishing company. Presently, I am doing work in another form in the world of cars and illustration. I would like to continue treasuring my childhood world of pictures and vehicles as a hobby.

末広治信
HARUNOBU SUEHIRO
P.107／P.115

1946年＝広島県に生まれる。1970年＝デザイン学校工業科卒業後，アートセンター入社。1972年＝テクニカルイラストの道を志願。1976年＝フリーとなる。JAAA会員。
連絡先＝〒272 千葉県市川市鬼高3－8－7
☎ 0473(70)8321
＊笑う，怒る，悲しい雰囲気のある顔をもった自動車。特に夜のトラックの顔には度胆を抜かされたのが小学生の頃だ。メカに興味をもったのもこの頃であったと思う。だが実際に自動車ととりくんだのが24歳を越えてからでありギャップも大きく大変であった。子供の頃に感じた，あの鋭い視線をなんとか表現できないものかと苛立ちまぎれに取り組むがやはりこれからが課題である。

Addr : 3-8-7 Onitaka, Ichikawa-shi, Chiba 272
Tel : 0473(70)8321
＊ It was during grade school days that I was frightened by cars whose features expressed moods of laughter, anger and sadness, especially the face of the night truck. It was also during this period that I became interested in mechanical things. However, it was after I was over 24 years old that I actually dealt with cars. It was, therefore, difficult with this large gap due to the late start. Hereafter, my subjects will involve things whose sharp looks I felt when I was a child but could not express, irritating.

鈴木英人
EIZIN SUZUKI
P.52／P.54／P.150

1948年＝福岡県博多に生まれる。1971年＝グラフィックデザイナーとなる。1980年＝イラストレーターとしてデビューする。主な画集に『オン ザ サニー・ストリート』『南カリフォルニア物語』『サウスワードバウンド』『アメリカンロードショウ』『イーストアルバム』があり，その他数多くの広告イラストレーションを手がける。
連絡先＝〒249 神奈川県逗子市新宿3－1－7
☎ 0468(71)5317
＊のりものは，ぼくにとっては風景だ。おもにアメリカの街並を描いているので，道があると，そこには車がある。写真で街並を撮ると，必ずといっていい程にのりものが写る。車であったり，モーターサイクルであったりするが，それは絵の中に良いバランスを作ってくれる。ぼくは，そういった街並を描いている。アメリカ中を撮っている。だから今までに数えきれないぐらいの「のりもの」を描いている。

Addr : 3-1-7 Shinjuku, Zushi-shi, Kanagawa 249
Tel : 0468(71)5317
＊ Vehicles are part of the scenery to me. Because I primarily draw American city scenes, there are cars on the streets. You could almost say that in all the pictures of cities, there will be vehicles. The cars and motorcycles help to produce a well-proportion balance in the pictures. I drew such city scenes while capturing the inside of the United States. Therefore, I have drawn an uncountable number of vehicles.

摺本好作
KOSAKU SURIMOTO
P.116／P.118／P.119

1936年＝三重県上野市に生まれる。日本大学理工学部建築学科中退。1955年＝模型飛行機製作記事を「航空ファン」等に連載。模型界に名をなす。バイクに乗り始め，1968年＝MCFAJのレースポスターがきっかけでこの世界に入る。ルポが多い。著書『日本一周ツーリング』『僕の駆ったバイクたち』。JAAA会員。
連絡先＝〒176 東京都練馬区早宮2－21－13
☎ 03(931)2012
＊僕はバイクが大好きで自分でも駆る。どこへでも入っていけるこの気軽さと一体感がすてきで，年と共につながりが強くなった。ルポの体験から，イラストは見て感じて描きたい。バイクと人間の関係が好きでテーマは自分で捜して歩く。1984年の日本一周は，大きな力になった。文の力もかりて，一冊にまとめる「本」書きが，今一番おもしろい。現在，7月完成に向けて，『鈴鹿8時間耐久オートバイレース』を執筆中!!

Addr : 2-21-13 Hayamiya Nerima-ku, Tokyo 176
Tel : 03(931)2012
＊ I am crazy about bikes and even ride one myself. This lighthearted feeling and the feeling of being of one to be able to go anywhere is great. The link has grown stronger with the years. From my experience with reportage I want to draw on the subjects I see and feel myself. I like the relationship between man and his bike and have gone searching for themes. The tour trip around Japan in 1984 was a great help. Borrowing the strength of writing, as well, I have compiled them in one book which holds the most interest to me at the moment. The Suzuka 8-hour Endurance Auto Race will be coming soon.

高荷義之
YOSHIYUKI TAKANI
P.30／P.43／P.45／P.142
P.144／P.146

1935年＝群馬県前橋市生まれ。1954年＝高校卒業後，小松崎茂氏に師事。1954年＝小学館学習雑誌でデビュー。今日にいたる。画集；1972年＝『電撃ドイツ戦車軍団』（主婦と生活社）1982年＝『高荷義之アニメイラスト集』（徳間書店）1986年＝『高荷義之イラストレーション──タミヤ・ボックス・アート・コレクション』（徳間書店）
連絡先＝〒371 群馬県前橋市古市町1－43－20
☎ 0272(51)5490
＊当初は機械を描くのは大嫌いだったが，えり好み出来る身分ではないので注文が有れば描いてまいりました。プラモデルの箱絵を手がけるにいたって，ほとんど全部が乗物の絵になってしまい勉強もしなければならなくなりました。今は無い昔の兵器，どこにも無いロボット等，難しい所もありますが，描き馴れたせいか近頃では結構気楽に描いています。

Addr : 1-43-20 Furuichi-machi, Maebashi-shi, Gumma 371
Tel : 0272(51)5490
＊ I hated drawing machinery in the beginning, however, one can not be too particular. So, when I got orders related to them, I drew them. I had to study in order to deal with the box art of play models of which almost all of them were pictures of vehicles. Sometimes there were difficult works involving old weapons that could not be found today or robots that were not available anywhere. However, perhaps because I have grown accustomed to drawing them, illustrating them has recently become fairly easier.

武田育雄
IKUO TAKEDA
P.25／P.136

1950年＝兵庫県津名郡東浦町に生まれる。1968年＝兵庫県洲本実業高校卒業。1968年＝㈲カラーテックプロに入社。1970年＝㈱TSP創設に参加。1976年＝フリーのイラストレーターとなる。1986年＝JAAA入会。
連絡先＝〒107 東京都港区赤坂4－2－23 赤坂エミネンス中川403
☎ 03(584)2774
＊乗り物といっても陸，海，空とあるわけで，今回のカバーイラストでは空のもう一段階上層部（宇宙）をテーマにトライしました。虚無の空間の中へ生命力あふれる若いセクシーな女性，SFっぽい21世紀のピーターパンを描いてみました。

Addr : ♯ 403 Akasaka Eminence Nakagawa 4-2-23 Akasaka, Minato-ku, Tokyo 107
Tel : 03(584)2774
＊ There are land, sea, and air types when you speak of vehicles. I experimented this time with another category above the rank of air (space) as the theme. I drew young, sexy women overflowing with life in nothingness space and SF-like 21th century Peter Pans.

常味真一
SHIN'ICHI TSUNEMI
P.132／P.134／P.137

1954年＝東京都杉並区に生まれる。1973年＝東京工業高等学校卒業。1984年＝浜野エンジニアリング入社。1985年＝フリーランスとなる。
連絡先＝〒182 東京都調布市深大寺北町4－20－10
☎ 0424(83)9403
＊子供の時からの乗り物好きです。イラストより模型少年でした。友人などからは機械好きだと思われているようですが，機械というより乗り物に動物的な感情を感じています。特に自動車，自転車，鉄道が大好きです。イラストは始めたばかりでこれからどうなっていくのか，「とにかくガンバロウ」これしかありません。イラストを始める時に大内誠氏に大変お世話になりました。先輩の方々，これからもよろしくお願い致します。

Addr : 4-20-10 Jindaiji Kitamachi, Chofu-shi, Tokyo 182
Tel : 0424(83)9403
＊ I have ever liked vehicles since I was a boy, though, I was more of a play model fan than an illustrator. My friends and others thought I liked machines, while contrarily I could sense more of an animalistic spirit in vehicles then in machines. I especially love cars, bicycles, and trains. Having just started in illustrations I have no idea of what is going to happen. There is nothing to go but to work hard. I am greatly indebted to Mr. Makoto Ouchi who helped me a lot when I first got my start in illustrations and I would also like to extends best wishes to all of my superiors.

豊島信彦
NOBUHIKO TOYOSHIMA
P.26／P.38

1951年＝神奈川県横浜市に生まれる。1970年＝神奈川県神奈川工業高校産業デザイン科卒業。1970年＝日本デザインセンター入社。1972年＝仲條正義デザイン事務所入社。1975年＝なんとなくフリーのイラストレーターとなり、現在に至る。1979年＝JAAA 入会。
連絡先＝〒241　神奈川県横浜市旭区南希望が丘65－6
☎　045(361)8186
＊私がイラストレーションなるものを知ったのは高校のデザイン科時代。卒業後、日本デザインセンターに入社して、自動車のことを何も知らないのにメカのイラストレーションを描き、そのまま現在にいたっている訳です。いろいろ寄り道をしましたので、のりもの中心の仕事内容ではありませんが、描いていて楽しいのはのりもののイラストレーション。子供が絵を描くのと同じ気持になれるみたいですから……、締め切りさえなければ。

Addr : 65-6 Minami Kibogaoka, Asahi-ku, Yokohama-shi, Kanagawa 241
Tel : 045(361)8186
＊ I've come to know what would be an illustration since the days of my high school design courses. When I started to work for the Japan Design Center following graduation, I drew wechanical illustrations without knowing anything about cars and have proceeded that way to the present. Because I sidetracked here and there, the main substance of my work does not concern vehicles, however I enjoy illustrations of them. I want to draw pictures with the same feelings as that of a child's-as long as there is no deadline.

中島　秀
HIDE NAKAJIMA
P.92／P.110／P.128／P.151

1950年＝高知県高知市に生まれる。1973年＝明治大学商学部卒業。在学中より矢野富士嶺氏に師事。1979年＝フリーとなる。JAAA 会員。
連絡先＝〒252　神奈川県藤沢市亀井野410－8
☎　0466(82)9638
＊自動車関係のテクニカルイラストを中心に仕事を進めていますが、今後は車以外のもの、またテクニカルイラストにとらわれず幅広い仕事ができるよう心がけています

Addr : 410-8 Kameino, Fujisawa-shi, Kanagawa 250
Tel : 0466(82)9638
＊ I have been doing work based on technical illustrations related to cars. In the future I would like to do a broader range of work outside illustrations of cars and technicalrelated fields.

中村　信
SHIN NAKAMURA
P.33／P.38／P.41／P.64
P.150

1934年＝和歌山県田辺市に生まれる。1952年＝上京、阿佐ケ谷美術に学ぶ。その後、馬木工房、東京アドデザイナースを経て独立。1972年＝㈲アバンアート設立。1979年＝朝日広告賞イラスト部門表現技術賞受賞。1979年＝JAAA 入会。1986年＝『映画のイラストレーション』(仮題)を出版予定中。
連絡先＝〒104　東京都中央区築地4－2－7 フェニックス東銀座302　アバンアート
☎　03(545)9889
＊車のイラストは、小冊子『スバルの歴史』を描いたのが始めて。以後スバルばかりにかかわって、車の透視図や車のイラストをいつの間にか描くようになった。現在は車の仕事は少なくなった。機械などの精密描写よりも、雰囲気のある風景などの方が自分には適しているようだ。車にも表情があって、冷たかったり、暖かかったり、つかれていたり、輝いていたり。そんなものが表現できればいいなぁと思っています。

Addr : Avant Art ♯ 302 Phoenix Higashi Ginza 4-2-7 Tsukiji, Chuo-ku, Tokyo 104
Tel : 03(545)9889
＊ I first began car illustration drawing for the pamphlet, "The History of Subaru". Drawing only Subaru from that time on I was, before I knew it, drawing perspective drawings and illustrations of cars. Work related to cars has at present declined. Meanwhile, zestful landscapes seem to suit me better than the precision delineations of machinery, etc. Cars also express emotions. I think it would be great if we could express feelings of coldness, warmth, tiredness, and joy in them.

中村安広
YASUHIRO NAKAMURA
P.50／P.58／P.124

1952年＝東京都渋谷区に生まれる。1972年＝育英工業高等専門学校工業デザイン科卒業。リズム時計、レイ・デザインに工業デザイナーとして勤務。1979年＝フリーランスのイラストレーターとして独立。1979年＝東京デザイナーズ・スペースにて個展を開く。1982年＝JAAA 入会。著書＝『走れ!!チョロ Q』(グラフィック社)
連絡先＝〒115　東京都北区赤羽台1－6　赤羽台団地53－418
☎　03(907)8836
＊デフォルメするにも、しやすい車と、しにくい車があります。勿論、好きな車は、思い入れがあるので、難しくてもなんとかカタチになります。特に60年代の車は、みんな個性豊かで大好きな車ばかりなので、デフォルメしやすく、ノッて仕事が出来ます。しかし、そういう仕事ばかりが来るわけでないのが現実で、やはり最近の車が多く、似たようなデザインが多く、デフォルメすると、見分けがつかなくなるのが、悩みのタネです。

Addr : 53-418 Akabanedai Danchi 1-6 Akabanedai, Kita-ku, Tokyo 115
Tel : 03(907)8836
＊ There are easy-to-do and difficult-to-do cars in deformation, as well. Naturally, I have in mind the kind of cars I like and no matter how difficult I somehow get their shapes down on paper. Because the '60's cars all so rich in individuality and my favorites, they are easy to deform and I can do the work smoothly. However, it is a matter of reality that I can not always do this kind of work. Of course, the recent new cars frequently occupy my work. As many have similar designs, it becomes impossible to capture distinguishing features. This is one of my agonies.

永野清貴
KIYOTAKA NAGANO
P.51／P.52／P.65／P.68
P.117

1952年＝宮崎県小林市に生まれる。グラフィックデザイナーを経て、1978年＝フリーになる。
連絡先＝〒180　東京都武蔵野市桜堤1－6－4　恵泉　西－202
☎　0422(54)2067
＊モノごころついた頃から絵が好きで、毎日のりもの等を描いてました。それが今も仕事として描き続けられている事を大変有難く思ってます。それから、いつも私の身近にあったのりもの、それはモーターサイクルです。遥か昔、父の後ろにちょこんと乗っていた時から現在まで、モーターサイクルは私には無くてはならない存在です。

Addr : ♯ 202 Keisen Nishi 1-6-4 Sakurazutsumi, Musashino-shi, Tokyo 180
Tel : 0422(54)2067
＊ I have ever liked pictures since the time I can remember and drew pictures of vehicles and other things everday. As my job, I draw even up this day to which I am very thankful. Besides that, I constantly have my motorcycle near me. Since the time I used to ride behind my father days long past, I can not imagine myself without my motorcycle.

野上隼夫
HAYAO NOGAMI
P.36／P.40

1931年＝茨城県日立市に生まれる。1949年＝岡山二高(現操山高)卒業。1949年＝日立造船造船設計部勤務。1969年＝日立造船退社。フリーとなる。1983年＝銀座アートホールに於いて個展開催。『野上隼夫艦船画集』出版。
連絡先＝〒192-03　東京都八王子市中山3－18－13
☎　0426(37)7686
＊少年時代は、戦時中で、飛行機、SL を描いていました。戦後は進駐軍のトラック、ジープ、軍用車を、就職先が造船所だったため、それ以後現在迄は船を、考えてみればのりもののイラストを描き続けています。今後、時間が出来ればやってみたいこともいろいろあるのですが、なかなか時間がなく、毎日仕事に追われています。

Addr : 3-18-13 Nakayama, Hachioji-shi, Tokyo 192-03
Tel : 0426(37)7686
＊ I drew airplanes or SL during the war in my childhood and drew trucks, jeeps and passenger cars of the Occupation Forces after the war. Since then, because my place of employment was at the shipyard, I have drawn ships. There are many things I would like to do in the future if I have enough time. However, it is difficult to find the time as I am always under work pressure everyday.

野口佐武郎
SABURO NOGUCHI
P.69／P.99／P.104

1921年＝旧満州奉天生まれ。1944年＝多摩美術大学デザイン科卒。1946年＝イラストレーターとして制作活動。1985年＝STUDIO of ILLUSTRATORSの主宰。JAAA会員。
連絡先＝〒158　東京都世田谷区等々力4－3－3
☎ 03(704)7222
＊JAAA展に作品を出品して、他の作家の作品を見る事が最も楽しい事です。日本の作家の水準が段々上昇してゆくのが見える様に思います。

Addr : 4-3-3 Todoroki, Setagaya-ku, Tokyo 158
Tel : 03(704)7222
＊ When I display my work at the JAAA Exhibit, I enjoy looking at the works of others of which I think the standard of Japanese artists has gradually risen.

初谷秀雄
HIDEO HATSUGAI
P.21／P.39／P.85／P.89

1947年＝栃木県足利市に生まれる。1971年＝フリーランス・イラストレーターとして独立。主に、クルマ、その他のメカニックなイラストを手がけてきた。作品に対してはリアル＋ファンタスティックな面を常に心がけている。これからは、更に、イラストのほかに、工業デザインの分野に力を入れ、自分自身の夢を一歩ずつ実現させていきたいと思います。JAAA会員。
連絡先＝〒166　東京都杉並区高円寺北4－5－3
☎ 03(338)1959
＊幼いときから、自動車や飛行機のスタイルに興味をもち、のりものの絵を書くことが大好きで、そのときからカーデザイナーになるのが夢であった。そのため、毎日、絵を描きつづけてきたことが、現在の仕事につながっています。これからは更に、夢のあるのりもののイラスト、又はデザイン画を描いていきたいと思っています。

Addr : 4-5-3 Koenji Kita, Suginami-ku, Tokyo 166
Tel : 03(338)1959
＊ I have an interest in the styles of cars and airplanes since a tot and have loved drawing pictures of vehicles. I dreamed from that time on of becoming a car designer. So, in order to become one I drew pictures everyday. My present work is related to this. I look forward hereafter to drawing more illustrations and designs of dream vehicles.

福田哲夫
TETSUO FUKUDA
P.88／P.89／P.90

1949年＝東京都生まれ。1967年＝東京都立工芸高校デザイン科卒業。1967年＝日産自動車株式会社設計部造形課に入社。1973年＝千代田デザイナー学院講師。工業デザイン事務所、環境デザイン事務所に勤務。1980年＝JAAA展（～85）。1981年＝第15回SDA賞を受賞。1985年＝A&F株式会社を設立。現在に至る。JAAA会員。
連絡先＝〒104　東京都中央区銀座1－14－12　銀座114ビル　5階　A&F株式会社
☎ 03(561)1951
＊未来に姿をあたえる………「テクニカルイメージイラストレーション」。物からの発想ではなく、未来からの発想………「アドバンスデザイン」そこには夢があります。心のときめきがあります。そして無限の可能性がひろがります。私はこれからもイラストレーションを通して素晴しい未来づくりに挑戦していきたいと考えています。

Addr : A&F Co., Ltd. 5th Fl., Ginza 114 Bldg., 1-14-12 Ginza, Chuo-ku, Tokyo 104
Tel : 03(561)1951
＊ Giving form to the future⋯ "Technical Image Illustration". It is not conceived from objects ; it is conceived from the future. "Advance Design" —— it holds dreams. It holds the throbbing of the heart while endless possibilities spread out before us. I want to take on the challenge from now on to build a fantastic future through illustrations.

穂積和夫
KAZUO HOZUMI
P.30／P.31／P.32／P.125
P.145

1930年＝東京都中央区に生まれる。1953年＝東北大学工学部建築学科卒業。1953年＝松田平田設計事務所入社。1958年＝フリーのイラストレーターとなる。ファッション、車などのイラストを主に手がけてきたが、最近はシリーズ「日本人はどのように建造物をつくってきたか」全10巻のイラストを担当。「法隆寺」でサンケイ児童出版文化賞受賞。JAAA会員。
連絡先＝〒154　東京都世田谷区下馬2－8－4
☎ 03(410)1161
＊自動車専門誌ではなく「メンズクラブ」など一般誌にクルマを描きはじめたのは恐らく僕が最初だと思う。60年代前期のアメリカのカタログのイラストレーションに魅せられたのがきっかけで、1969年には「自動車のイラストレーション」（ダヴィッド社）を出版。1976年には、クルマ、飛行機などを中心に歴史的シーンを再現するドキュメンタリー・イラスト作品の個展を開く。最近は建築物が多く、のりものはあまり描いていない。

Addr : 2-8-4 Shimouma, Setagaya-ku, Tokyo 154
Tel : 03(410)1161
＊ Probably it is me that illustrated cars professionally not for an automobile specialist magazine, but for general magazines like "Men's Club", etc. Captivated by the illustrations in the American catalogs of the early 1960's I published the book, "Illustrations of Automobiles" in 1969. In addition, I held a one-man show of documentary illustrated works that reproduced historical scenes focussing on cars, airplanes, etc. (1976). Nowadays buildings and similar subject themes occupy the majority of my work, while those of vehicles have declined.

細川武志
TAKESHI HOSOKAWA
P.64／P.65／P.87／P.101
P.131

1943年＝広島県呉市に生まれる。モーターファン美術部を経て1971年にフリーランスのイラストレーターとして独立。JAAA会員。
連絡先＝〒187　東京都小平市小川町1－969－18
☎ 0423(43)3757
＊テクニカルイラストの取材で色々な単体部品のメカニズムを見るとそれを考えついた人の頭の良さに頭が下がる。センスあるイラストを見ると頭が下がる。色々な手法にチャレンジしている人を見ると頭が下がる。顔を上げて何かひとつこれはと思えるものが描けるようになりたい。

Addr : 1-969-18 Ogawa-cho, Kodaira-shi, Tokyo 187
Tel : 0423(43)3757
＊ When looking at the mechanisms of the various unit parts in the collection of data for technical manuals, I bow my head to the marvelous know-how of the people who conceived them. I bow my head to illustrations that have good sense of composition. I bow my head to people who challenge various techniques. Thus, I want to draw well enough in order to lift my head for something.

牧田哲明
TETSUAKI MAKITA
P.115／P.123／P.130

1935年＝愛知県豊橋市に生まれる。1959年＝愛知大学経済学部卒業。その後商事会社、デザイン会社等に勤務。1968年＝フリーのコーポレート・デザイナーとなる。1976年＝近代日本美術協会々員。1977年＝JMAC入会。1979年＝JAAA入会。
連絡先＝〒440　愛知県豊橋市花田町字築地41
☎ 0532(31)5822
＊私の学生時代は自動車、ヨット、自転車に興味を持ち、草レースに出たのが、のりものとの深い関わり合いの始まり。現在は魅力あるイタリア車とモーターサイクル、特にアルファロメオ、アバルトなどコンペティショナルの美的な逞しさに心を奪われ続けています。これからも、モータースポーツの歴史的な背景と自分のもっている車に対する情熱を、油彩、木版画等で表現し、より一層、共感できる絵画的な作品を描きたいと思います。

Addr : 41 Tsukiji Aza, Hanada-cho Toyohashi-shi, Aichi 440
Tel : 0532(31)5822
＊ Having an interest in cars, yachts, and bicycles since my schooldays, I began my close relationship with vehicles in local races. At present I am continuously captivated by the beautiful power in gorgeous Italian cars and motorcycles, especially in the competitional Alfa-Romeo and Abarth. I hope to capture in the future, as well, the historical background of motor sports and my passion for cars in oil paintings or on wooden plaques. I want to draw painting-like works that can further bring forth a response.

森 優
YU MORI

P.55／P.103／P.126／P.129
P.150

1942年＝東京都千代田区に生まれる。広告代理店のチーフデザイナーを経て，フリーランスのイラストレーターとなる。1980年＝JAAAに入会。1984年＝銀座松屋にて個展を開く。1981年＝日本デザイナー学院の講師となる。著書「クラシックカーを描く」「エアブラシの技法」。1986年＝10月銀座松屋にて個展を計画中。
連絡先＝〒140 東京都品川区東大井5－9－7－607
☎ 03(472)5592
＊クルマそのものを描き始めて十数年がたってしまった。クルマそのものが好きだった事から，それを描く立場になったが，なかなか思うように描けない。最近はエアブラシも技法の中に取り入れてみたが，表現技術が多少拡大したように思う。クルマそのものはフォルムを変化させ得ないので色彩的に何かデフォルメ出来れば良いと思うが，これがなかなか難しい。

Addr : 5-9-7-607 Higashiooi, Shinagawa-ku, Tokyo 140
Tel : 03(472)5592
＊ It has been many years since I first began drawing cars. I like cars, however from the perspective of the illustrator, it is rather difficult to draw as one pleases. Recently I have also incorporated the air brush technique in my work which has somewhat expanded the scope of expressive delineation. Although unable to induce alterations in the form of cars, the results would be good, I think, if they could affect some kind of color deformation, however this is quite difficult.

安田雅章
MASAAKI YASUDA

P.32／P.118／P.152

1954年＝東京都千代田区に生まれる。1977年＝日本大学芸術学部美術学科卒業。1977＝㈱杏文堂にデザイナーとして入社。社内の人気者となる。1984年＝JAAA入会。同年フリーとなる。1985年＝新車のハイラックス・サーフを事故により半年で廃車，同年，発作的にビッグホーンを購入。以後そのローンに苦しむ。賞罰なし。以上。
連絡先＝〒160 東京都新宿区荒木町23 NF メゾンインターフェイス111号
☎ 03(359)6869
＊のりものとの第一遭遇は，3歳の頃自転車のギアに指を挟まれ，とにかく"痛かった"ことが印象深い。第二遭遇は，8歳の頃身事故をまのあたりに見た。第三遭遇は，17歳の頃，単車との異常接近。"これが青春だ"と真剣に思っていた。現在，のりものとは，つかず離れず非常に良好な関係を保っている。以上の様な事が自分のイラストに，どう影響し，今後どの様に展開していくかは，誰にもわからない。

Addr : ♯ 111 NF Maison Interface, 23, Araki-cho, Shinjuku-ku, Tokyo 160
Tel : 03(359)6869
＊ My first encounter with vehicles was when my finger was caught in the bicycle gear at the age of three. Anyway, the pain left a strong impression on me. The second encounter was when I happened to see a serious traffic accident at the age of eight. The third encounter was my unusual close relationship with my motorcycle at seventeen. I seriously thought "this was the prime of my youth". Even to this day inseparable without breaking our bond I have kept an extremely good relationship with vehicles. No one can tell how the above events will effect my illustrations nor how they will develop in the future.

矢野富士嶺
FUJINE YANO

P.82／P.85

1940年＝東京生まれ。1958年＝京北学園卒業後，モーターファン誌に1年半，以後フリー。JAAAには創立以来の会員。
連絡先＝〒253 神奈川県茅ヶ崎市小和田3－9－62
☎ 0467(51)7922
＊60年代米車のカタログのイラストには，全く感心させられ，当時はどうやって近づこうかという日々だった。商業イラストの場合，ある程度，時の流行に合わせねばならぬ事もあるが，それとは別の努力もしてみたい。

Addr : 3-9-62 Kowada, Chigasaki-shi, Kanagawa 253
Tel : 0467(51)7922
＊ Deeply impressed by the illustrations in the 1960's catalogs of American Forces' cars I reflected everyday on how I could approach that level of excellence. In the case of commercial illustrations there is the factor f having to somewhat keep up with the trends of which I would also like to make an extra effort.

吉田和弘
KAZUHIRO YOSHIDA

P.91／P.107／P.113／P.138

1942年＝千葉県舘山市に生まれる。1966年＝日産自動車退社。1969年＝桑沢デザイン研究所卒業。自動車会社宣伝部制作室，イラストレーションスタジオを経て，1974年＝フリーランサーとなる。JAAA会員。
連絡先＝〒240-01 神奈川県三浦郡葉山町下山口1238
☎ 0468(75)3337
＊自動車の構造図が仕事の中心ですが，これからは，いろいろなものを手がけたいと思います。

Addr : 1238 Shimoyamaguchi, Hayama-cho, Miura-gun, Kanagawa 240-01
Tel : 0468(75)3337
＊ The core of my work involves the construction plan of automobiles. In the future I would like to try my hand at various things.

イラストレーション　ザ・ビークル
(ILLUSTRATED TRANSPORTATION)

1986年6月25日─────────────────初版第1刷発行

Cover illustration─────────────武田育雄　**Ikuo Takeda**
Artdirection─────────────────乙部信雄　**Nobuo Otobe**

編　集　グラフィック社編集部
発行者　久世利郎
印刷所　錦明印刷株式会社
製本所　錦明印刷株式会社
写　植　三和写真工芸株式会社
発行所　株式会社グラフィック社
　　　　〒102東京都千代田区九段北1-9-12
　　　　電話03(263)4318　振替・東京3-114345

定価　　3,800円
ISBN4-7661-0382-3 C3071 ¥3800E